Open up the Sky

A Poetic Conversation

Heather Cardin and *Rob O'Flanagan*

Vocamus Press
Guelph, Ontario

Written by Heather Cardin and Rob O'Flanagan
Some rights reserved
©①$②

Cover images by Heather Cardin and Rob O'Flanagan
Some rights reserved
©①$②

Cover design by Jeremy Luke Hill
Some rights reserved
©①$②

ISBN 13: 978-1-928171-03-4 (pbk)
ISBN 13: 978-1-928171-04-1 (ebk)

Vocamus Press
130 Dublin Street, North
Guelph, Ontario, Canada
N1H 4N4

www.vocamus.net

2015

Heather Cardin
For the Babi poet Tahirih, who died for the emancipation of women; and for my mother, who loved words and used them beautifully.

Rob O'Flanagan
To old friends with Saskatchewan connections.

Acknowledgements

Heather Cardin
Thanks to Robbie, who, through the process of this creation, changed from being a casual acquaintance to a friend. Thanks also to Keith Bartlett and Valerie Senyk, who offered early encouragement. Thanks to Mitzi O'Flanagan, for enthusiasm and love. I'm grateful for arrivals and departures, because they remind me of why my heart can have many homes. I'm grateful for my mom teaching me to read at age three; my family, who are often willing to listen; some wonderful friends. Lisa Brosseau, you're my star. Linda Kirby, Jack McLean, David Erickson, the Ottawa Writers' Group: thanks. Thanks, Jeremy, for helping this work find its readers. Thanks, Daddy, for trying poetry. I am grateful, always, to God.

Rob O'Flanagan
Without the conduit of online social networking, its power to connect old friends and allow others to comment on and encourage dialogue instantaneously, this poetic conversation likely would not have happened. Special thanks to Valerie Senyk for her ongoing support and encouragement, and to the community-building and unifying principles of the Baha'i faith for establishing lifelong friendships rooted in mutual respect, shared struggles, and devotion to the independent investigation of truth.

Preface

by Valerie Senyk

Heather Cardin and Rob O'Flanagan first met through the Baha'i Community in Saskatoon when they were youth, but their adult lives took them in separate directions. Over a span of more than twenty years, they each pursued their individual writing. Rob published two books of short stories and performed poetry accompanied by various musicians or his own electronic music. Heather published her poetry in journals and authored four books of non-fiction.

    Eventually Heather moved back to Saskatchewan to an acreage with her husband, teaching school to preteens, while Rob moved to Guelph, Ontario, working as a reporter and columnist for the *Guelph Mercury*. Then one day, through social media, they started to talk – through poetry.

    Heather posted a poem, and Rob found within it his own poetic response. Heather responded to his poem with another of her own, and again he reciprocated. And so it went. Together they created a book's worth of delectable and emotive poetry, a loving and dynamic dialogue between friends, matching line for line, sentiment for sentiment and image for image – two voices, sensuous, playful, attempting to define the indefinable.

Note on the Text

In order to make both voices of the poetic conversation distinct without being too intrusive, Heather Cardin's verses have been set flush with the left margin, and Rob O'Flanagan's verses have been slightly indented.

Open up the Sky

A Poetic Conversation

Heather Cardin and *Rob O'Flanagan*

Open Up The Sky

Silence is sometimes broken
sound to past selves
still finding forward into this time
where love is still the reason.
I shed my brown skin for spring
while rushes whisper more than lullabies
and memories rush breeze
through pores: the soul's osmosis
filters each 'was' and 'might have been'
'til time dissolves and we are found
back in the place of hallowed ground,
the soft sere prairie song,
this ancient future rune.

And silence is sometimes spoken
in brushes of wintered fingers.
Our past springs forward,
a whine in the wind singing:
"This is you and was you."
Swept in the rush of green
we seek a closer we
not broken.

We see it, too, in skeletons
where grain fell into bins
more clear than transience,
blue flax against a southern sway,
canola sun against a far flung
orange moon. Still, the drunken
remnants of a wooden door
invite us into centuries

beside the tracks. Still, across
the itchy plain we see that
shadow land of sailors who
remain, hold fast to metal,
sky and something more than gold.

What was, a ruin.
What might have been, a home.
Some prairie song hoped for
in the gullies and plow furrows
where you leaped and swept in
sage-scented breeze
mumbling your own lullaby.
"Sleep, dear one, sleep/
The earth your bed/
Souls wing here in willow."
What might have been home is ruin.
Gunshot tore the big sky,
bled soft songs and hung
sulfur where sage was.

The silent harvest bound
to sibilant past where
once we stood beside
a derelict spire. I miss
the place of prayer where
rain fell only rarely but like
bread, and suddenly,
this kiss, this harvest bliss
until the silence, once again.

Open Up The Sky

I miss the blue flax seas
of raft-play and soakings.
Narrow channels poled
to bits of navy glass
and bones of floral China,
where the leaning
bin stood tipsy in dry winds.
Beyond, a ghost elevator with
moaning throat of pigeons.
Reach that and you've reached
the sailor's world end
and ate and drank
what they served:
distilled rain water
filtered through
a maze of rafters
saturated with harvest hope
and ladybug skeletons
and grain dust that wanted
to be bread and bred in the belly.

It's in the bones, shards more than these necessities
of history, cut glass calcium like the chandelier
of an eternal sky. Here's the script: someone soft
meets something softer, the heat of sweat
trickles down the spine of solitude.
Here's a guess: these great pillars of the western sky
stand, still sentinels, rounder in the sweep
of touch. Our hands against the boards,
our skin and breath prepared for earth.
Not yet, not yet again, not quite yet. No dirge is sung
for this return. Still, we hearken

to the nubbled rub of thumb on stubble,
breathe in the scent of fibre, sigh,
and turn our backs back east towards charade.

    Here's the script:
    From deep stratum,
    soil seeded with bone,
    arrowhead, hammerhead,
    clay piece, iron piece, bead.
    Mostly tools of necessary slaughter.
    The kill.
    Farther up, scattered bead,
    perfume bottle, doll's hand.
    The after people, the breakers.
    He always said:
    "There was a graveyard that corner,
    plowed under. Don't ever take your
    sift and shovel there."
    What corner is that?
    Never you mind.
    A corner calls you
    through the plow furrows
    and stubble.

And see the man who crouches there, tests the silt
as drifts on horny palms. A palimpsest
of women conflate to sun and wind
by skin leeched over ruins. Sometimes,
a winter memory of sod
builds under muted colours
faded into water, dried.

Open Up The Sky

From these same sprang cities, small,
but built by rivers, built south and north,
pile o' bones, this yield to arboreal ranges
we can't call our own.
Something digging true, a spot against
a sunswept heap. The silky sky,
the sundog, moondog mist to tell
us why we still exist. And still they
itch, like phantom limbs and ghosts,
spirits in our slough-filled skins
and drink. There is no water here,
no kill-site beckons from the bank,
and there, the light, and there, the deer,
and once again, a night sound,
distant. This is the call,
so simple and so deep unearthed.
Shattered, stretched and still,
they lie against the land,
the compost of a choir,
a bag of flour and of earth.

Through the roof, the circle of day,
first auger load. He crouches,
breathing harvest dust,
new wheat burying knee and thigh
before the shovel flies.
Ladybug wings erase debts
in a banker's ledger.
New jeans, sneakers, rifle.
Each year the same warning:
"You can lose a hand in those blades.
Keep your shirt tucked. Think. Think."

Between loads, dream a jigger's path
through alkali gullies, bone glare on a
slough's shore.
Mind fly down to where the bathers take
the salts, where non-swimmers float
and praise the Earth's floating properties.
This is the simple call: When the fields are in,
wash away the dust, taste the vanished sea.

Eddies, gullies.
The sound of an insect she can't name
found in hot cleavage under old bone buttons,
cotton. Drives slowly past the watershed,
watches birds gather. Is that a pelican,
is it a fish? Who gives it this name,
this blessing? The swimmer rises from
the loam, arches to a passing
cloud. Grasshopper rests between.
At Manitou, the kicker slides,
earlier than heat. Later, she will ride
that one last dipper, lift higher
than a shelter belt, laughter
to the purple skies. Mirrors
reflect shadowlands,
the blurred horizon undulating,
a centrifuge dipped in
her fresh honey.
Parched, they gather.
Parched, they drink.
They shade their eyes with lavender,
hands brushed with
seasalt residues and pollen.

Open Up The Sky

Caught in currents, they float
upstream to life, find liquid buried.
Deep, shale and stone. Eddies.
Gullies. Bone.

    A small place.
    A small place set apart.
    Not much to see at night
    but the sky light waves
    and winged things at
    the lantern.
    So many beings here
    and in the heavens.
    God lived on this island
    for a time, made those mountains
    of crystalline bone,
    blew the fields clean of scrub,
    imprinted so many beings
    in stone, and walked away,
    casting a long shadow over
    the northern shore,
    which is seen from heights
    in small places apart
    when the light is right and dancing.

Here are tales of gods, dancing sky
at night. But only when it's cold.
Only when the silent cold curves
body like lines cast over water.
Cold reaches bony fingers
all along his naked scales

and sheds through breath,
visible after dancing,
winter's tumbleweed beside
the resting plough. Hands
cup faces turned to heavens
where dance shines and wavers,
water in a sky made winged
by weather. A slight glance
in any direction. A glance
over that peculiar hard crunch
beneath the bones and bark
where spirit painted
silver in the frozen mist.
A pause, the dancing sky,
and fire.

    A hot wind in the sky.
    Wings of lashed poplar
    stretched with holy tarpaulin.
    As good a day as any day
    to fly.
    The air at steeple height
    is hot still but will get cold
    when the wind lifts you
    to gliding sandhill crane heights.
    Watch, with bird's eyes, the
    approaching storm,
    the tumbleweed in the
    spiraling cloud,
    and hope the lashings
    hold.

Open Up The Sky

Trees are acts of grace. Sometimes spindled,
sometimes shorn, a canopy of rustling.
Poplar turns quickly in the fall,
reminds us all to watch. Listen, once more.
Nothing splits
but sound or silence. Choose.
Pretense is a vortex. When you dance
by trees, the spiral spins you out.
It's a helix, a multiple suspension.
Reach the apex. Keep climbing.
It's better than dreams,
this message. Weightless.
Turn again, glimpse
mystery brought to ground.
Something delicate begins.
Something stable reaches.
Look! An anchor.
Now, lightning. Expect wet,
pray. Crane upwards for Beauty.
Cathedral forests pierce
waiting, God's permanent umbrella.
Then, wind.

The mad ascender's ladder.
Best rungs at the top,
dangerously springy and new.
You have to be nimble to
get up there.
But get up there.
Listen to your feet,
check your breath,
talk to fear in

grandmother tones.
Remember you are still
attached to the ground.
Up there you see the path God's
breath makes over the
golden sea, and the
calligraphy in a magpie's belly.
Up there you see the source of
the river beyond the boreal
and the confluence of pilgrims'
winding cuts over the plain.
Yes, it looks high from the ground,
and it is.
But up there you feel
a smaller part of it all,
and that the ground
was never yours alone.

This we know: like Rumi, we whirl,
flotsam, this dance of centuries;
long before us, the circle curved itself,
silk on sky. A tasseled frost
reflects the jetsam grain.
Aloft, see dancers,
shadow hieroglyphs, pounding feet
hollering hurrahs from deep
in their earth's belly. Echoes,
above, from the raucous ones,
moon-speakers, sun-wheelers,
utterance in language
more familiar than blood. Breath.
Mystery and its brother, desire,

Open Up The Sky

furrow as we till.
Wave! Raise a spirit-hand
to those who float and fly.
Closer, closer.
Here's a prairie dervish, come to
twirl. Tumult subsides. Breathe,
easy. Weep, squint, kneel. Rise.
Again, take the bridle, drive. Look up.
Spin. Spin. Wheel and turn.
Dust rises small signs to lost ones,
yours, and mine.

Lost ones were found here,
their bellies storing
grains of homes left.
(There is always an open door
in the brute world.)
Some faced naked the
absence of peace,
painted themselves
in slough mud,
became cracked clay conductors
for mystery and begged the sky
dancers to descend.
Mouths sealed and still as stone
they stood, some absorbed by
the earth, others dancing off their
itch.
And flaked by the breath of God,
washed by the land's sweat,
those caught by the swirling wind
found a new river home.

Their footpath – littered with clay pieces
and tears – the future's highway.

And where they walked, they planted.
Keeping time, the lingering legacy
of distant trains, inaudible music
become foursquare, a polka,
a toss of chicken feed on the down beat.
The hum of bees in beans,
scrub corn, the scrabbled search
for tubers, rumours in
blemished earth. A tin cup,
a shape of sinew, a curve of breast
in a ragged dress once blue.

Or is this romance, the down dirt
glamour of remembered
happenstance?

There's a woman eating clay,
swollen, or that one,
there, holds the needle
tight between lips and teeth
made hard by kisses.
When was denim born,
or a lip plugged with
chew and spit,
tobacco, smoke,
the first tough flake.
The shit.
The lazy day, the hazed hard
maybes. (The open door

to sleep, the dream.)
When eyes open, the world begins
before the light, and tarries.
Eyes closed, music, yes, perhaps.
And what of salt?
On wings of south-bound
geese, hunger, eyes on sparrows.
Wind, the careful drift. Suddenly, a field,
and mercy. Home, and mercy. Home.

    As they walked, they talked,
    eyes open, through ghost homes
    owned and operated by wind.
    Pelt stretchers stacked in a dim corner.
    Pressed tin ceiling brushed with soot
    over cold pot-belly stove.
    Scattered fur trade brochures.
    "Make your fortune in taxidermy."
    Windowless clapboard watched over by ancestors
    ornately framed and hung on peeling walls.
    Outside, failed ginseng patch,
    a stoneboat that lost the ground war,
    ensnared by rosebush and sickly poplar.
    Beyond, the lone pine of a still-born grave.
    The song of sparrows, moan of wind
    in which are woven jump-rope rhymes.

Step up to the threshold, a hewn stone.
You may have to bow your head;
step with care. Someone welcomes there.
A soft glow, a scent of something warm.

Berries, bread, a honey-pot.
In the corner, a familiar shape
kneads, stretches, kneads.
She looks up in greeting. Worn,
what was that which she was humming?
A country tune, an old air?
Here is patchwork, here a doily
and a thrown shawl. A patina of age.
Outside, the sound of a nightbird
spills: here the dusk
entrance into an embrace,
stoic thread upon the warp
of place. Where is this yeast,
the warm butter melt of wealth?
A good year. A table's set,
a plate, a bowl hoed and harvested
before the winter fell.
Sit, partake. Even the weary
hold the fiddle fast,
and sometimes speak, and dance.

    They bow their heads,
    hike skirts, lower trousers.
    Clenched teeth suck air
    rarefied by old work, new
    pleasure.
    These ghost homes, shacks and bins
    are for lovers now,
    for breaking the tedium
    of intimacy.
    From corner to corner
    histories are held,

of the callused hands
that tightened the strengthening
wire, of the fist that punched
the dough, of the child that scrawled,
"I lived here" in the closest wall.
Twist, knead, scrawl.
Messages left for lovers
who are pulled to places
belonging to sparrows,
ghosts and wind.

Sometimes there's wonder.
All stops. It's not unusual, a sound
or scent, lilac or a nursling sign of spring.
It's the nail, the whinny,
sight of a small creature pokes
a timorous head out of a hole.
"Nuisance", he growls, but she hides
a smile, roughs calluses across
a nearby head. A small child tips
a grin. All stops.

Capture this, the wheat poem,
the threshing poem, the sky and sound
poem, and hold nothing.
This intimacy, a brush, a straw broom
leaning against a barn once painted red.
This pause, her brow against him
as the anvil of his day. He the caliper,
she, his screed. Wonder at tongue

in palm, groove slid silently to
where their start belongs.

    Marty, Buck, Hank, Glen,
    Porter, Johnny, Roy, Conway.
    Hurtin' and floating,
    the scratch of vinyl
    on the porta-player.
    Her drifting songs
    drifting to the top of poplars,
    the muffled soundtrack to a
    wavering horizon, upon which
    ride phantom buffalo, and oh
    the heart hurts as she dances
    in back of a too-small clapboard
    once painted daffodil, into which
    were pressed too many children.
    "I fell into a burning…" and drifting
    up on a skip, the scent of lilac,
    the taste of caragana blossom.

The foundation's shakin' for the fiddler
and the fellas in the hall.
The rafter's rockin' while
she tells him 'bout her Grandmama,
hair so long she couldn' brush it out
'fore milkin' came along. She says,
"Honey, that's when I learnt my
favourite word." Smiles and hollers,
"Jamboree!"

Open Up The Sky

Starts kickin' up them pointy-toed boots,
clickin' them red heels.

He buries his self right in her, then,
an' all that whoopin'
and hollerin' keepin' the beat.
Have you ever seen the rodeo?
Hey, hey, hey.
In the kitchen they kept
the heat. He said, "Your pastry's
flaky, baby," when the music
simmered down.
She laughed, "I think your tractor's
sexy, baby, it really turns me on,"

and they powered down the throttle hard
till the stars were settin' strong,
ate pie and traded deep-moon kisses,
whoopin' outta tune. Uh uh uh.

A mighty voice was captured here
or was the voice shot, like an antelope,
while sipping from a frozen slough?
Long before the highway and railroad
and rodeo, the path of a gaunt horse's
stumbling retreat in a light dusting of snow.
Long before the walk-a-thon, the barbecue
and the Indian show.

A stolen steer,
an encroachment one way
or the other.

Someone starving or starved.
A mad thing called private property.
The stone marker by the highway
says less than the crows and God's
whistle in the poplar forest near.
You read it once taking a piss
in the ditch but can't remember
its history or who told it.
But these jingle words remain:
"Let's all take in the show.
It's the Golden West Road-up,
Take your family, and go."

At night, a kettle whistled.
Sometimes, they took it outside,
hoped the smudge would keep back
biters and boiled black coffee.
Spiked. Molasses and sage,
arms wrapped 'round things
thick and thin. Arms wrapped 'round.
She could never get that particular
perfume out of her hair,
washing in the bucket back of the house.
Rubbed down with hard soap.
Not too near, a calico store.
Not too far, a small school. Primers
for ABCs, 1-2-3s,
memorizing fair English gardens
with daffodils,
winding dandelions in chains
at recess games. Quoth the raven,
said she, watched a hawk

Open Up The Sky

wheel over a dip in the land
near a coulee, spat out marbles
from her mouth and sucked up
river stones. Barefoot river girl
in pigtails carries a bucket full,
hungry. Forward, backwards,
bracken, a bracket before moving
west again. And west,
still moving. Moving.

    Honeysuckle twig stuck in the jaw.
    Needle and pliers boiled in a pot,
    no one had the nerve to use.

    "If you leave it, it will sprout
    leaves and yellow flowers. Like
    the guy with the pear tree in his
    throat."

    Certain extractions require
    an old bachelor, gut-sour
    with Copenhagen, toughened
    by solitude, with stories
    of three-legged dogs,
    great bucks turned to men
    after the trigger was pulled,
    black bear in a trapper's shack.

    "It'll scar, but you need scars.
    Drink some of this."
    A chokecherry spirit for the pain.
    "What the hell happened."

"Road hockey."

Soon, floating in the head,
prone on a split log bench,
a dragonfly darting before his eyes,
threatening to fly off with him.
A sensation like a single leaf birthing
through the skin of his cheek.
Soon there will be a tree
where his face should be.

"This won't hurt."
One quick thrust at the jaw,
and the sapling, bloodied at the trunk,
was uprooted.

"Drink some more of this."

So you think you're tough?
Try this. Try a small opening
like a sweet princess pea
(later she will paint and call them
flora). Try swollen varicose
veins of pushing. Breech
means more than solitary,
leads to rivers of red
under skin so slight
a light feather brushed
turns it white. Push.
In winter, swelling subsides
under ice, teeth crunched
and ground fine to shards.

Open Up The Sky

Can you count? Open,
open again, grind, scream,
wider, wider. There are so
many liquid places, so many
shades.
What is born? Milk,
gum, a sapling scored
by a hard knife. Sap.
Another notch in his belt.
Another word for death:
croup. Cough and spit,
a midwife's ambulance.
Boiled water, pinched nipples
hard to bring out
after birth. Animals eat it
up. Cracked but never
broken, the shake
of muscle wrapped in a cotton
caul. Afterwards, candle wax,
the soft murmur of life.
This, the weld, the canvas,
the joint of hip to bone.
Keep counting.

    Eye level to the surface of the river
    vision partly under/partly over water.
    Clarity with the blink of an eye.
    She sees, through distorting drops,
    a day when there will be a child.
    It won't be tossed the way she was tossed,
    but, with tiny tummy to palm, skimmed
    partly under/partly over the surface.

Watch and learn if she's a sinker or a swimmer.
She has learning that's never been words,
things to say to a little one's ears
that are all ears,
especially when floating
and supported by a digger's arms.

She surfaces for a breath,
a canoe's wake cresting at her chin.
There will be a child.
She'll wrap her on
and hike to the mill
with the canister of soup.
The men's ears are numbed by noise,
but maybe some would listen
to the learning she's never shared.
How you say this word is, sir-prize,
and this is what it means.
And this one here is ab-zorb,
And this is what it means.
They will eat less noisily
with a little one near,
set aside their grunts,
and cursing and glare
and maybe listen then.

Every day a bucket.
Bucket lunch, bucket down the hole,
bucket water, bucket full o' new potatoes
from the gravid garden.
Milk pail, slop pail, pail of peelins
for the pigs. Chicken scratch,

Open Up The Sky

leg scratch, head scratch,
crotch scratch. Hole digger,
earth digger. Well digger,
what we don't have here is
a gold digger. Gold grows
above ground. A boy named
Clay starts coming around.
He don't want to be a digger,
ain't interested in no holes.
He wants bucket full of north
northwest where rumour says
it's best. It's all she knows,
till someone kicks the goddam
bucket. Does she glance
back, going down the weary road?
No one knows. No one knows.

    A poplar is a look-out tower.
    A tractor a tank.
    A bin is a safe-house.
    A cattail a torch.
    Purple gas in a bucket
    is a bomb.

    "I gotta take a piss."
    That's Daryl,
    who grew up to drink
    and take his dad's job in parts.
    He did it no hands,
    because it's hard to hold
    yourself and a cattail torch.
    In a state of blessed relief

he relaxed and let an "aaa"
slide out his throat,
and touched torch to bucket
and the bomb went off.

A pump is a hydrate.
A bucket row the townspeople.
Two maples at the head
of the row a fort's wall.
The towering flames,
are the towering flames.

A requiem is not played on an accordion.
A dirge is not played on a fiddle.
An elegy is not written in any script but tears.
No bagpipes, no flutist. Grief is
percussion. Metal: it's metal. Wood: it's wood.
The bucket, overturned, is a bell.
A bell is inscribed with script,
alphabet fired. The script is wind.
Wear a visor when you stare into the sun.
Eclipse is circular, a cupped palm around
phosphorous, a smell of sulfur.
Descend Jacob's ladder into
a waterless heaven,
haul the rope hand-over-hand.
Signal alarm, ring and ring.
All hands, all hands.
Grief is an empty casket.
Grief is the forlorn wail of the siren at noon.
Grief is an early tombstone
carved, *requiescat in pace*,

Open Up The Sky

on quarried stone. Grief climbs
above steeples. Grief is felled
in the silence of a boy whose name was fire,
its last sound of mercy stifled. A bell.

Grief, in woods.
Grief, in reeds.
Grief, in fields.
Grief, in cars.
Always sulfur on the lips,
and the salt of tears.
Some get the pipes.
Most, the throat song,
the scream that won't
come out.
The throat song,
the mute scream
at a locked heaven.

Pleasure, in woods.
Pleasure, in reeds.
Pleasure, in fields.
Pleasure, in cars.
Always sulfur on the lips
and the salt of sweat.
Some get accordion,
others wild jazz.
Most, a cry stuck
in the throat.
Not quite grief.
Not quite ecstasy.
Some shed tears,

some laugh,
at the crack in heaven's door.

Mute.

She wishes, always, she could cry,
let salt weep to the gloaming spot,
the throat throb space,
the thick place between thorax
and crown. She wishes for the sigh of
deep release, the coming into clearings.

Locked, her throat is an instrument
where even death, a mighty metal,
cannot turn his key. Nor water nor heat
can melt this salt, the gathering of verses.

Locked, only return to life
returns her to the willow,
the wet brook. Locked,
there's only burning,
desire behind crusted eyes,
something struggling to swim
out into a waiting world. Locked,
shadows dance in the vixen stream.

Healing. Healing comes in waves,
the throat opened by the touch
of a willing tongue. Still, no cry.

Mute.

Open Up The Sky

The momentum of the coming.
The unready are readied.
Those schooled in hunger's wail,
who know the ways of new
eyes, ears, feet, skin
spring to action.
Cedar chests fling open.
Sweaters, sleepers, mittens,
outgrown and keepsaken,
thrown back into circulation
as links in an unbroken
craft of love.

A knitter's art is for
the growing, for the arrived,
for the embraced.
Take these for your coming.
They weren't made for a box
or a frame. You wore them,
and so will she.
And in a needle's click
more adornings come.

It's in this Beauty.
Tissue, fabric. Gauze and colour.
Words: vermilion, ambergris,
weft. Skin is patchwork in a mirror,
each stitch a fine etch held
by the same plain sea.

Is this what it is,
to be woman,

to be a man in this place?
Is this what is,
fabric's translation into grace?
Soft down holds her weary neck,
a feather in a cap. Soft skin,
velour, a comb. Ebony?
Cloissoné to hold thick braids
from falling to her waist.

Burlap, once worn, now
holds taste. Root cellar,
jelly jars, the shade of raspberry.

Gingham, lace.
Thread like penny candy
on a shelf. A milliner,
a machine rocked and pedaled.
Sometimes feet beat time
and create a seam,
design like cast iron of the maker.
On the wall, brocade fades in pleats
and there, beside the stairs,
wool wears a wooden floor
in all the old familiar ways.
A portrait, an upright piano,
a candelabra, still burning.

Yes, yes,
an unbroken craft, a link:
knit, purl, knit again,
embroider love in layers.
Colour. Taste.

Open Up The Sky

He sits at the pipe organ,
the last living thing
in a church that lost its flock,
believers and doves.

He hammers out something
abstract and breathy,
to clear the dust
and cumulative severity
ingrained in keys and peddles
and guts.
A drone to correspond
with the storm mountain
approaching from off
the curve of the earth.

There may be angels here
but the music doesn't
draw them down.
Instead, the click
and moan
bring the rumbling
black mountain and its bolts
near, and it is only he
who seeks refuge here.

Nearby, a cathedral, painted. Imhoff,
not really a chapel,
a stone wall, a wood floor, a chancery.
Moving space. Whitewash. Inside,
stations of the blessed
Cross. Outside, stations of the blessed

Grass. God's own pipes reach up
to blessed sky, a ring of cotton.
Nothing more, nothing less.
They say the word: "*Ave, Ave.*"
From somewhere, whispers
wash on a weather wall,
a pastiche, permanence.
This is how to say, "Believe,
and it is." This is paint,
this the nave, connected
to the navel of all that is earth,
sky, and every paean in between.

    Her thing is distance.
    It's what her limbs and lungs were made for.
    Out on the tractor roads and grids,
    where neighbours are beyond
    a stone's throw, she can hear
    the cheering in the sweep
    of wind over grass and grain,
    in the chickadee call and cricket chirp,
    in the wild applause of the ruffled grouse.

    She finds her own paths,
    sloshes through the shallow
    sloughs, through the ghost
    yards and stubble trails, down
    sage gullies and along
    intestinal creeks that wove around
    every obstacle to carve out this valley.
    Her feet thrumming an
    old ground beat, over which

Open Up The Sky

is layered throat songs, and
the constant din of an earthy
rally cry: "Run, run, run. You
are nearly there, where
spirit and body are one."

She knows the universe is plural,
knows it as she breathes,
knows distance, no matter
how she runs, will find
her garden. Love's lost
design? Within. Within.

She knows she's winter's
child in summer, summer's
any other time. She sings
cold frost starred silhouettes
of barren branching
trees. Her body, her leaves.

Sometimes she forgets,
sees distances as small,
sees solitary shrunk.
Tunnel, speed and grid,
the narrow pelvic width
of earth on down the line.
She knows: the jig, this
journey, spin, the run
is mercury time. She cannot
break, she will not break.
Oneness lies within. Within.

He is far out there,
deep in the scrub lands,
with the whitetails and antelopes.
Another thin brown patch
in a many shades of brown tapestry.
Is he the only being out here
asking why, in this vastness,
there is another brown patch
of dust and water walking?
He must be the blade of some
telling, the shoot of some pattern,
the sift of some sky message,
some heat message, some bone message,
through which the patchwork is defined.
Or just another shadowed
stitch in a quilt made by ice, wind
and fire, a stitch if frayed or broken
would unravel nothing.

It's not that he is half of something bigger,
or that she is. There's no numbers to this sky,
no counting blades of grass nor sheaves.
There's no wayside where they whisper
more than size. There they are in mudflats,
buffalo memory, cabbage moths lifting.
Aurora, dips, gullies. There they are,
now walking, then at run, sometimes
stopped.
In silence.
Just looking.
Looking.
When cloud dissolves, shape is there,

Open Up The Sky

inchoate. Being, ephemeral, seeming,
not enough. Not quite enough,
until, in stillness, her hand finds his.
Softness. The harsh soft of truth finds
their work, shadows, spirit-land walks.
Yes, there are senses. There are.
Sometimes, though, they close their eyes
to stand silent in the wind.
This is the romance of truth in hand.
This is this.
This is.
This.

    This is this.
    A burial mound for stones.
    A burial mound for bones.
    A ghost rumble of skulls
    bashed in and tongueless buffalo.
    A drive-in movie theatre
    with its neckers and pant-dippers
    driven out, and a sawhorse
    stuck on the diagonal.
    From this high point
    your echo reverbs
    over fifty miles of
    short grass, green in spots
    where a homesick cloud
    decided it was time to cry.
    And you see the wave of your
    best coyote call, your best, "Hello,
    are you out there!" skipping like
    the perfect stone over a glacial

river's gouge and retreat.
And why is that forest up high there?
And where is the rodeo when you need it?
And somewhere in one of these
three-quarters ghost towns
you are bound to find
a good used cowboy shirt,
embroidered with sheaves and
a rearing pony.

Every time they think it's over,
buffalo gone, something small appears
to whisper, "Not yet, not quite yet."
The thing is, they realize, they have
to stand still to see it, to hear it.
Too much movement and the shy one
will run. Too much, heavy boots will
trample a small sign of spring.
Every thing emerges from this ground.
It's when they wait that they can name it.
Ladybug, crocus. Patchwork is a hologram,
a stalk of wheat tipped against,
her hands cupping a blade of grass.
A whistle right there in the palm.
A startled grasshopper.
No see 'ems in a cloud.
They drive through. Later,
she finds creatures at the back of her neck,
etchings. He washes the windshield
and thinks of skin.
Whitetail, brome, inflorescence a name

Open Up The Sky

for shining. The world sleeps, they slip.
The skin of the world wakens for this.

    It can be supposed that
    Sitting Bull sat up here.
    It can be supposed he stared out
    at the wavering eastern horizon,
    as you do, on this ridge at the roof
    of the uplands, and pondered
    what was coming next, like you.
    More glass that shoots shafts
    of sun to the height
    of the sandhill crane.
    More coffins that play
    music. More men who take
    and can never take enough.
    It can be supposed that this
    felt something like home.
    A miniature Black Hills,
    in future times overrun
    by goatee wearing bikers
    and models in leopard skin bikinis.
    Watched over by those monster
    presidents that turned a mountain into
    mantel piece kitsch.

    It can be supposed he was up here.
    That he walked, stared out, marveled,
    as anyone would, at the glacier's slide,
    how it skirted this rock and
    left this forest crown.
    There is a trail still,

up from Wood Mountain,
five days on foot or slow horse.
A society trims back the
grass from the markers for now,
until the buffalo return.

And what of velvet? A brave man carries weapons
in crushed velveteen above a faux fireplace
on fake wood panelling. I've tried not to look
at bevelled mirrors reflecting
an anonymous Chief broken
by coloured water behind upholstery.
I've tried not to look at a pigtailed
wampum child, someone's imagination
in buckskin and leatherette
wearing feathers and beads bought
at the Sally Ann. Tried not to look at
interior carpet, a chartreuse pretense
of grass, not to look at synthetics,
chemical collaborations
with trade names like "Flying Indian"
or "Winnebago".

I've listened to my Metis friend Cheryl,
danced at Batoche, worn dangly earrings
handmade in China and
asked please to forget how to say
wannabe. I've tried not to watch
them wheel churches down
highways past Battleford sentinels.

Open Up The Sky

I've friends wandering sagebrush hills
to gather wild blueberries. Wild roses
wither when picked. Gathered and picked.

And what of Avon callings?
Corvette Stingray aftershave,
Southern Bell bubble bath,
Oktoberfest beer stein,
Indian princess perfume.
They asked her to judge
the beauty pageant
on the reserve.
She knows beauty, that one.
"They know me. They're
my friends and my customers."
There's a China cabinet
full of her collectibles,
tokens of her income
supplementing years,
tokens of the hobby years,
the need to get out of the house years.
"It's worth a shit-load now,"
a former mocker of the
product line now asserts.
She received watches,
travel clocks, charm bracelets,
commemorative pins for
freshening the air,
making glacial blue the toilet bowl,
keeping ladies lady-like,
and men musky.

It all piles up after forty years
of Avon callings.

Remember the shop beside the lake?
Or maybe it was north of there, closer
to mosquito belts where yellow starts
by July. South, that place we went
inside 'nd they tried to sell us moccasins
made of smoky moose hide. As if!
Dreamcatchers in every dollar store,
baby. Curios. I'm curious all right.
The time you went out in summer night,
stole windchimes right from under.
Dingalings swinging
in prairie moonshine.

Seriously, she can't wear lipstick
anymore, it just runs into lines
round her mouth like old ladies
write with needles.
She gets a run in her new
fishnets, baby.

Seriously,
what's her tune,
Buffy Sainte-Marie?
Starwalker was a friend of mine.
Uh huh.

I believe the drum, sometimes,
when the moon is high in a summer sky.
I trace a circle with the red tip of my index,

Open Up The Sky

bite hard when someone's riding.
Every bottle means something
sweet, baby, like *"je reviens"*.

Still running.

Frequent travelers
on the Fort-de-la-Corne Freeway,
in search of a kill and a drink.
There used to be a store,
where fields merged with forest,
for chips and rifle shells.
A stop on the road to slaughter,
with birch wood fire you could
sink into, beaded muck-lucks,
smoked Jack, cigarettes, firewater.

It used to be all there was,
now there are diamonds,
and the merchants
of Antwerp and Tel Aviv
know the name of the place.

It depends on what you're looking for:
forest, freeway, sparkle
of water or a jewel. Start from furs,
end up digging. It depends on what
you're digging for:
fame, notoriety, take your pick.
A lot comes from under ground.
Far enough gone, almost anything

can hide. Strip, and it's gone.
It depends on what's worth
squinting for in clouds. You get
a crick in your neck, glance down
wards. A trick of light
tells a different story. You can
smell it, there's something
there. You can't put your finger
on it. Some people just can't stop
digging. Some people just can't stop.
Uranium, gold, what does
any of it matter? Unto dust shall
we return, or maybe some
are made of sand and struck.
Lightning strikes and opens
up the heart, fissures
'til we're made dumb.

        You are crossing the narrows,
        drifting and dragging
        a funeral boat of buffalo bones.
        Looking for an eddy and landing.
        A dead-fall raft of snarled
        roots and branches.
        You are saving a few bones
        from certain death.
        Tired from the kick and haul
        you wrap an arm
        and go with the current,
        along dune islands
        above carp bottoms
        past the upstream nudists

who come to the shore
to see what is dead
in the water.

Not so long ago government paid a white guy
to go to the south end of a northern lake and teach
people to plant gardens. Every morning sun rose.
Boys set off, brown hands on a rudder,
for a nearby island garden. North means a forty-five
day growing season, surrounded by fir and fur.
North means digging roots
overlooking Reindeer Lake, an army of mosquitoes.
North means watching Martha run after Jimmy
with a cast iron pan in her hand, almost airborne,
shouting, "Hastam, Hastam."

Inland northern water, lake like a sea,
trees an army, vegetables harvested
after new summer became old.
Waves rise past the old outboard.
Can't paddle fast enough.
You lose direction. Where's north
or south without a current?
In the gloaming a curious deer
watches antic two-
leggeds foraging for food
while horse-flies bite hard,
thick. Smudge and driftwood.
Time, again, for digging.
Over there, a lonely wood cross.
Over there, water. Over there,
digging and digging.

Over there a marble tablet.
Someone died sometime,
small pox, old age, heart,
drowning, gut shot,
horse kick or trample,
war, fire, cave-in, fall,
and is planted here
to grow at a future time,
an end time, undetermined,
when the conditions are ideal.
It's a good garden
a nice bunch of seeds taking root.
Kneeling gardeners squint
at the clouds and think
they see something riding there.
Then, the clang of cast-iron.
Shouts of bloody murder.
Were any of these
planted by a frying pan?

Then there are the laugh out
loud times. The holy roller
bootstrap kickback chewin' up times.
The milk of magnesia oil
of old lady castor oil times.
The hail stone gall stone
soap stone times. The black
ice when you're driving to
St. Louis times. The later times
when he's steering north
and you look up to the bridge
above buffalo bones times.

Open Up The Sky

The cast iron statue, sunny
side up times. Marble, pollen,
stamen, jiggin' times. Town
halls, crooked bells, old well
times.

Sometimes the garden gets
eaten times. Big fat old gopher,
rabbit stew times. Raccoon
on the back porch, bear
in the nuisance ground times.
Laughing out loud, laughing
till you wipe tears from your
loving eyes cackle like that old
crone times. Hitchin' up denim,
hitchin' the wagon, gettin' hitched
up times. Blowin' dandelion floss
times. Laughing times. Laughin'.

Something to chew on his walks
around the home quarter.
A length of straw, a twig,
a palm of wheat.
He spoke to himself about
the present government
and the state of his people,
about the current troubles
and the troubles that were.
Always with his hands clasped
behind the small of his back.
Always way out to the corner
of the land, sometimes farther

when the troubles needed
a lengthy monologue.

Contemplation sudden, a tumbleweed
of the unexpected. Extemporaneous,
a prairie Shakespeare. Duration variable.
Couldn't see the point. New-fangled
gizmos. Recently needs drugstore
specs to read *The Western Producer*.
Veteran of auctions and bad coffee.
Skeleton rust steps up on a vehicle
seen better days. Logos on his cap
change from time to time, once a decade
or two, fade like sunspots on the back of
hands. Gnarled and fractious,
short shrift for locomotion. Listens to news,
calls her "the wife", or simply
"Mother". Turns laconic into volubility,
uses elbow grease to scrub grease.
And so it goes.

Here, a shrine finder
with a witching sense
for the charm spots.
Aligned with prevailing grace,
seeking settings most womb,
most blanket, most arch, most monument.
There are mercy places everywhere.
A clearing by flowing water
with a branch canopy.
A sudden mound on constant flat.

Open Up The Sky

A limb or tooth of granite spared.
Finding there the stations,
the medicine wheels,
the worn ground of
constellation gazers,
the monk's labyrinth.
Always some evidence
of sacrifice and the scent
of prayer and blessing.

There's a sense of the divine,
grasp of a stripped bough
knows more of depth,
finds a well and keeps it.
The divine of birthing:
a mallard opens
to reveal an egg,
soft beside the water.
The cloaca of earth
yields mysteries as a child
traces greengold on
the soft down head
of a feathered mate.
Fingerlings, a chameleon whispering.
Mercy: a bud opens,
a sweetgrass braid left upon
a stream and stone altar.
An arbor made of feathers,
wickerwork and spiderwebs,
the long stretch of tarmac
under the felt moon sky.
Much is made of the shadow world.

Still the song is mercy,
mends hearts in a weave
of scented smoke.
Alleluia, Alleluia, and Amen.
If you kneel, you may find
and stroke translucence
with your breathing.

If you kneel, there is only time.
Ticking away in stones' silence
in dust waves over bone
in measured lapping of
hawk rippled water.
This is how you breathe,
through cheek heat
and cool beads on the
back's furry small,
waiting on nothing
hoping on nothing
sage whispers amen
up a nostril, a crow
calls the approach
of dusk, and there is
so much time.

If you kneel, a magpie will know you
as a shining thing, and may pluck
you up in its talons and take you
to its stash, which may include
a wedding ring and rosary.
It is always good to be so
still that even the smartest

and most skittish bird
assumes you are inanimate.
In this way, you are led to
treasures.

Stillness at centre of the wind
stretches even the most experienced
of sinners. Everything sudden:
anticipation, force, duration.
Then the quiet nucleus for all
the waiting whispers.
Collections are not things,
but flesh. Better than a bird
fetching you back is the same one
upon your shoulder. Wings folded,
the pulse in a sparrow's chest.
They say St. Francis was a nest.
They say his song could be heard
even in silence. Even in wind.
The pipes called, invisible
scattering angels called.
You can fly, they say, even
when anchors rust into sub-
terrain streams, when you are
centred in the eye.
There are no hurricanes,
just lashings tearing at green rope,
the coil of hay in a field
where truth hunches over
a feathered saddle in wind.
This being torn. This being.

St. Francis in her garden,
the train above.
She loves both
the rails and saints.
Once she found wheat
growing between the ties
as her jays and cardinals
bathed below, and hearing
her father's song from down
the silvered bend,
she saw him running,
in one of his better stories,
to an open boxcar,
riding to some form of work,
or at least a view of other lands
or seat at other storms.
Let's say he planted this
seed here, overlooking her
garden.

Sometimes she dreams of catching crabapples as they fall.
After they bloom, before the great pots boiling jelly or sauce,
before a fire or a cauldron, before an early touch of frost,
before gathering roots, before making.
When she wakes, there they are, all the flesh and pink
of them, all the winking stems. Nothing much at core,
yet somehow seeds. Grafts, pruning, change of shape.
Sometimes she dreams of sweetness.
Variety, spice, the hard crunch of picking.
Here, she sings a mother song, a knowing song,
a gather ye song. If she had one, she'd tie her straw
bonnet under her chin with a blue ribbon,

Open Up The Sky

a wicker woman gathering pippins in a bucket.
Out of the corner of her apple eye, her daddy
tips his hat west. Sun, squint, the sound of apples.

Under five, six feet of snow
everything rests, including
barbed wire and roads.
You take the Arctic Cat,
she the Mercury.
Some things don't rest
in the winter, and for those
there are shacks.
Barrel stoves and instant coffee,
whitener, sugar, army bag, brittle
copies of Stag magazine.
The hunter's staples.
She worries there are mice in the bag.
You assure her there are – 10 of them
at the end of your feet,
curious and hungry, cold to the touch.

You set traps with Cheez Whiz and peanut butter
in a mobile home. It never moves,
just sits through snow drifting past windows
in plastic. In summer there were
tent caterpillars by the thousands.
One of the children was frightened
till you showed her you could squish 'em.
Your friend reminded you:
"They're all God's little creatures."
True. Keep squishing.

Listen to traps snap shut,
sometimes a dozen a night.
Chaff feeds hungry ones till spring.
Leavings, scraps.

A trip to auction where
he shouts, "Sold,"
and you take home someone
else's goods. Recycling foreshadowed
by foreclosure. False fronts not only
for pictures. Empty bins are side-
lined by remnant silhouettes.

Traps, leavings, freight-damaged
jars from other places,
prune juice, sauerkraut.
Everyone learns to nibble,
fix the holes with something sticky,
Juicy Fruit, Doublemint that lasts
and lasts, no bubbles, the sound
of smacks. Traps. Leavings.
A gavel: going, going, gone.

    Before he lost his desire,
    lived too long for comfort,
    a road-trip was his prayer and learning.
    Cypress Hills for wonder,
    the Rockies for thanksgiving,
    the Badlands for perspective,
    the farmlands for abundance.

Open Up The Sky

He became unmoved,
closed the book of the road,
stored his tattered maps.
Travel became a danger,
the unfamiliar a threat.
He speaks of the mountains,
deserts and forests as
though things of the past.
You assured him there
were still prayers being heard
on the open road.

It's hard to hold yourself.
So much inside fighting you.
The visible scars, chin, eyebrow, scalp, knee.
Those are the easy ones –
the hockey cuts, the knife wounds, the infections –
the healing ones.
The deeper wounds whisper,
"No one listens when you pray."
Even out in this near desert,
where it is just you and Him,
you feel mute and invisible.
Who cut you so?

This town needs something
or the ground will take it.
A dinosaur discovery or UFO landing.
A starlet running away from it all,
an outlaw to call it home.
Where is the promised migration
of idealists with plenty
of hoes and shovels,
and a circle dance that will

make it rain?
Maybe just a meteorite
to level the playing field,
give us a fresh start
as a reservoir basin.

The thing is, prayers are whispers.

All around, past strip malls, urban sprawl.
Everything of wonder
seems filled in. Then comes
a moment when breath
renews: a grizzly sighting,
an honest-to-God raptor.
In the distance, a wheeling
wingspread leaves prairie behind.
At Banff, she soaks in hot springs,
closes healing eyes. Bright light
reflects off evergreens and snow.

She remembers a picture.
Her parents, young, in love,
1955, newlyweds, these same springs.
This is heat, this is the rightness of things.
There are valleys where board feet
are old and weathered, like them,
and spirit rises up to meet laughter.

Fruit blossoms delay, seem more like snow
feathers than potential for sweetness.

Open Up The Sky

Prayers are there,
but you have to listen into. Into.
Everything meets on these plains, yields
to mountains, snow, slow buds
on still naked trees.
This is good.

    Prayers are there, whispered.
    The stones hear them and rise,
    asking to be fulfilled as burial mounds.
    The creeks hear them and flow,
    promising soon to shed a bank
    and reveal old bones.
    The sky hears them and widens,
    telegraphing its storms for
    your safe-keeping.
    The valley hears them and
    lets the wind pass through,
    playing its music over long
    grasses and wolf willow,
    accompaniment to whispered
    prayers.

After whispers, she waits. This
expectancy, still wonderment,
hope for response. Wind, sail,
stream, bird, or distant whistle
of a train: floaters, time-keepers,
auras hover, teach her to cleave.
Does prayer, once offered, become a shout,
a butterfly in a tidal wave?

Is it a lost chimera in her mind?
Too many mysteries and symbols,
scripts in alphabets appearing
more and more
undecipherable
illegible
dangerous
like afterbirth.
She's the bee,
a hummingbird, all the small
chorus of sisters, sipping.
She gathers lilacs by armfuls,
waits. A hedge spirit:
Confirmation's
a shelter belt,
baptized by rain.

    A gradual pacifying.
    A single sad song,
    listened to again and again.
    Subtle flashes of yellow
    recognized as life.
    The mating wing-drum heard as music.
    Until there would be
    no more killing on
    her home quarter.
    The .22s and 12 gauges,
    the 30 ought 6, and 20/20,
    gifted to the boys of other farms.
    Soon, a sudden immigration.
    Whiskey jacks and meadowlarks
    ruffed grouse, prairie chicken, magpie.

Open Up The Sky

They ate what she scattered
and filled her remaining acres
with song, drum
and airborne acrobatics.
While all around, the bulldozers
scraped clean deer lair and fox den,
crow's nest and owl hollow.
But her green patch,
flashes and song,
flashes and song,
the hummingbirds sip the sugar water.
The cedar waxwings strip the mountain-ash
when it is time.

Some days she sits cross-legged
amongst beans or zinnias,
imagines she's hidden even from
the eternal sky,
and recites her prairie alphabet:
aurora, birch, coulee, daffodil,
everything, fox, geese, happiness.
Looking up, and across, anywhere but down,
she knows what she has not before:
sight and sound tell stories to intuition
that she can't find but that lands
like the butterfly over there,
and sips oblivious of her breathing.
Winged ones. Ladybugs can fly.
There is no need for names,
here in this garden,
startled by the sound of distant shot,
which brings her back from daydreams.

Summer, fall; she gathers and abides.
Gathers, and abides.

    With the sound of distant shot,
    her breathing quickens.
    Something is out there about to pierce
    a stillness as inconstant as field stones,
    frenetic as the hummingbird.
    Down beyond the netted gems,
    again the ghost bachelor comes up the road
    to court what he could never court.
    "Now you appear, you bastard!"
    She throws a spud that doesn't scare.
    Instead he hovers there, stubble fire
    and field smoke through him.
    His pockets filled with a man's mixture
    of jack-knife and rounds,
    washers, wires, coins and flints,
    that keep him grounded in the night wind.
    She lets him speak a moment to her instincts.
    In one quick breath she knows
    the body is fed by ground,
    but the heart's nourishment is in the air,
    and she follows him just far enough
    to see him fade in dusk's mauve horizon.

Following is a chinook,
a grace warm flood.
Wind before wet,
the garden pulse.
She licks lips. Salt,

Open Up The Sky

sugar, everything forbidden.
Love wheels and dives,
her beat the bird
dipping in the honey sun.
Hot, a burning day,
a melting day. All are
beggars. Beg for
night sky, shadows,
return to open mouth
still giving. Nothing
cool as water. The black
lake, slide, skin, soft
memory. Soft.
She comes up again for air,
a fish, flying.
She comes up again for wind,
and leaps, lands, splays.
She comes up again for stars,
sings lullabies to absence.
The solstice hooks her
into drowning. Everyone's
a beggar in the night.

    All are beggars,
    spirits in a broken world,
    out of place, a little lost,
    cupped hands
    closed eyes
    walking blind
    lead by song.
    Give us something!
    Some sweet fragrance

or melody in the air.
Open up the sky a crack
above the bluff
show us where we were
born and where we return.
The beggar's path from
stone to stone, on powdered
clay, in search of some
black water in a crack,
some honey drip from the sky.

That's what sun rises for,
if you wake to see it.
Crocus announces
and rustling shadows sing
each body moved to silence.
Genuflection, this worship
dawn and dusk,
this liquid more than
God's microwaves. That's
why we kneel:
because earth and sky
are there. She says,
the least we can do is
attend. A celestial party,
jubilation, aurora.
She's been north
and watched electric orbs
remind her. She's been
south, seen the harvest moon
rise over Qu'appelle.
Who's calling?

Open Up The Sky

Sunflowers turn east
to west, transubstantiation
in the work. Bread and water.
Bread and water. Bread, and stone.

Who calls? *Qui appelle?*
There's a grinding
in the wheel well.
The bearing is going,
but held since Minneapolis.
He's close to home, close to beginnings.
Not afraid of a breakdown.
He hikes up the sage hills,
where tuberculotics once
wandered with little breath
above the sanitorium,
their coughs carried
on a warm wave over the river,
sweeping back in echo
through long grasses, "Here
we heal. Here we heal."
He kneels, nose to ground
and clears his throat.
"Who calls!?"
Home. Home. Home.

She's invisible in long grasses.
That's the beauty of it: dissolving
into. This slow dissolution,
a journey without final destination.
All over the map, she

bypasses highways for grid roads.
They've been there a long time.
She likes grinding gears
where no one hears.
First is easy, at first.
The swath is narrow.
She knows she's ribbon
from the sky.
She shifts from grid to grid.
mood capricious as weather.
She tries to identify each scent
and when she stops, walks,
sidestepping guano in
an in-between dance.
The beauty shades of green
shot with yellow cry
"Yes" in insect calls:
Buzz, flit, sip, still,
once more round. She can't reverse
but why would she want to?
Going forward is where she wants
to be, to find
where she starts up.

    These are the roads he knows.
    The grids and dirts his mother
    flew over, in Parisienne, LeSabre,
    BelAir, Skylark. The ticklish lift
    in the stomach over the three
    humps, the rush of tall grasses
    brushing the window where he
    stared out, blurry eyed, past

Open Up The Sky

the solo pine of a stillborn's grave,
skirting the Carrot and the Stoney
hanging on to something,
then, on the crumbling highway,
peering over the seat
to read the needle.
75, 80. 85.
What was her hurry?
To shrink the gap
between town and country,
find solace in costume jewelry
and pub life. To speak instead
of listen.

Hazlet, Verlo, Piapot, Kincorth.
On the perimeter of the near desert.
He doesn't know these sand hills
or what made them, and won't
pretend to know.
Some knowledge was not delivered,
like the shame histories
or geography of scrub lands.
Dumont was down here,
a running marksman,
the buffalo tracker.
Sitting Bull, close.
A new people, nomadic
until the invention of
barbed wire and the
long reign of prejudice.
Other heroes might have been,
instead of Leif the Lucky
and Davey Crocket.
The conqueror's conquest.

The machine's progress.
The victors' histories
as taught by the submissive.

Names make us hungry. Belly-hunger,
bread-hunger, the hunger for memory:
nothing slipped away, everything intact.
Land as it was, sky as it was. No ghosts.
This is a hunger we cannot fill.
We eat and eat, and drink, and eat again.
Grain rests idle in grand collections on highways.
Oversized cartons, milk spilled,
times before "organic" meant more. More.
I still see her, sometimes, that woman
who eats clay. I still see her, a woman
in a circle dance who offers smoky tea
from an enamel pot. The woodstove,
until electric. I still see her, driving
hard and away, holding it together.
A rolling pin forms this crust of land
brushed by leaves. By leaving.
There's listening,
and there's listening. That's why,
the why of silence and of hunger.

I sometimes see them
the camp boys
the field boys
the track boys.
Cam, Dennis,
Brian, Mark,

Doug, Lance.
Experts at rail walking,
working an ax on deadfall,
fire starting, pit swimming,
horseplay.
Here we are skipping stones
And there, stuffing sandwiches
cheek to cheek to make time for ball.
Noon hour pugilists, flushed and bloodied.
Sling-shot marksmen.
Masters of the tree climb.
Always hungry for adventure
in back-alleys, burning fields,
roof-tops, ghost houses,
pool halls, drive-ins and clearings.
Hungry in body and soul,
forever boys balancing
on the rails.

Rails. At crossings, the fade-
in-fade-out
X.
Black and white.
Later, colour, signals,
speed and derring-do.
Journeys counting cars.
Wait while we count ninety,
two full of scrap iron, a garage sale
invitation: buy my rust.
Ghosts of men without women,
last spikes and first ones.
The Rocky Mountaineer

climbs seas of grasses
into ocean green, teal,
silver. Mountains, blasted.
Around bends,
white crosses hold faded
florals. Plastic.
Nothing and no one
can withstand this.
North or south,
CP or CN: take your pick,
take your acronym
and tunnel, blast, chip.
A famous song,
echoes of silence,
gold coasts. Gold,
steam, iron,
grain, 'til the last leg.
Specters, signals.

    Faded yellow the house.
    Steely silent the rails.
    Hurting the music.
    Icy mountain winds.
    She is tired of gambling.
    to sow or not to sow,
    To sell or to hold.
    Wheat or barley,
    flax or canola.
    Where will the starving be?
    Where the glut?
    So beholden to the air,
    sky, sun and belly.

Open Up The Sky

Ground damp.
Purse tight.
Sun retreating.
At a distant crossing
a whistle cries.

Sound announces morn
and evening. Sound is indigo,
violet, grey silhouette, a mirage
of water where sun slips
good night to sky, and sky
speaks in return: "Soon,
soon. Day comes quickly."

Sound is shadow:
Across her creek, a faint
lamplight drifts,
imaginations, movements.
Who goes there?
An ember, a figure slouched
near a dip in the land,
a tip of his hat,
something stirring.
Fire, smoke, a loon call,
a train call, a small prayer,
safety in a cry. She stirs,
holds the small one nuzzling
for her weary breast,
glances up once more
and finds shadow.
Soft, and lamp, and light.

Some are lost young.
Back country roll-overs,
drowning drunk,
playing with arms
or fire.

The stupid accident.
The horse shit luck.
Mischief gone horribly wrong
never to be righted.

Maybe some higher purpose,
a pattern, a point beyond
sky, beyond the confines
of grid, gravel and dirt.

There's no thinking it.
It's more in the nerves,
in the tenders of the belly.
This is what fields are for,
the snaking creek beds, the golden
waves and bone-bearing gullies.
To listen for the after voices
of your lost young,
to be swallowed by the
gapping land and told
in your veins where you stand.

There's surely elegy to it,
a form of peace. So slight
a memory, a smile, a quick turn
before last sound and crash.

Open Up The Sky

Unbidden, tears won't shed,
grief will not move from
the shattered throat of silence,
of whom to tell. Not so close,
yet not so far, a boy, a time
and place, a sudden meeting
with eternity. All day it rains
for him, for that one child,
for all the children we can't hold
and keep. Across the hills,
a swift and springlike breeze
reminds us of their names.
I send a prayer, and gather
lilacs in the rain.

    He found a bed of reeds
    and whispered his last
    breaths through them,
    a light wave and wake
    easing him through.
    The mothers' cries are
    still echoing there on
    the swampy shore,
    and paddles skip
    a stroke as though a
    hollow rests below the
    surface.
    Those who remember
    know it is a bubble
    in the shape of a boy,
    a pocket of air

left for those gone
under a third time.

He believed deeply
in his eyes
and in his throat
they never lied
That is where shore meets sea
that is where the rifle rests
that is my love and she sits.
Then flood
shot
empty chair.
His eyes failed him,
deeply.

Above ground, sky pours its libation.
Heat, melt from the icy heart
of the world. All sing a requiem,
da capo al fine. In memoriam,
we wet the world with no regrets,
the rising coast, our loss of reason.
Vehicles are instruments,
escorts from this liquid world
to some other kind of warmth,
the sound of water rushing
to the wound of the world.
We lift a glass in libation,
fill our veins with weary wishes.
Is there somewhere it's not raining?
Or does the sun, our ancient friend,
dance a misstep in eternal sky?

Open Up The Sky

At the end of the score,
the rousing sound of cymbals.

A dry quarter,
the rains bypass.
He walks out to confront the sky.
"Is it something I did?"

There was the Bonli girl
within walking distance
of a bluff's clearing.
A love broken so near
this ground, under this sky.

"Is that it? Is that why you
withhold your rain –
because her tears dampened
here?"
The sky answers with
a dust devil that takes
his cap.
"Is that a yes!?"

How do I, you, we, they
read the signs? How does he
know, the one who sifts sand
through callused hands
which way to turn, where
wind will go? How does
she, a spit of her index finger
raised to sky or drawn across

the face of a laden table,
the soft baby cheek,
the dust bowl, the scrap heap?

Testament is a kiss,
knowing simply wakening
to another day, another dawn,
another kettle whistling,
calling into every element
they can find rolled into love.
Just because they're young,
they will be old,
will look on stolen moments
by creeks and under willows
with music playing in their minds,
feathers tangled midst
the tumbled greygreen sage
like answers.

    The sign is the move.
    The grace in the action.
    Sometimes it's quick,
    a look left and right,
    a breath in stillness,
    and the planting choice
    is made.
    A certain sun warmth,
    the bend in a rock shadow,
    the carry of bird song,
    the speed of wasp flight.
    The only book on the subject
    is in the belly,

the only measuring devices
spirit and flesh.

Like making bread. They ask her,
how much of this or that.
Flour, yeast, sugar, oil, water,
salt. There's no cup to this.
Temperature is felt,
a drop on the wrist,
movement. To knead.
The tick of a clock,
the thump/whump.
Her art is what's not said:
a handful of berries, currants,
a sprinkle of seeds on warm dough.
The egg is warm as she holds it,
breaks, paints glaze.
Generations will try,
mix and fold. It's her wrist and hip
to make it true,
the right way, the strong way.
Everything rises:
Loaf, spirit, home.

Like making paintings.
They ask him: "What are you trying to say?"
He stands back, scans corner to corner,
stumped by the question.
He thinks: 'I'm not setting out to say.
I'm feeling my way.'

The materials have their nature
worn and weathered in the surface.
Farm family ruins,
found linoleum,
worn formica,
pressed ceiling tin,
sewing machine drawers,
commercial signs reborn.
Work it, work it,
sprinkle, nail, glaze, draw,
mix and fold.
"Sometimes the back
is just as interesting as
the front."

They ask again: What are you trying to say?
He dredges thinking from unthinking.
"I want to say what's gone,
what's in the ground,
what's got us to this point.
It's about the land
and a tortured beauty."

And the tortured century,
from Picasso to Pollock to
Prozac. Okay, okay.
What of pastel and pearls?
Cashmere, matched sets?
Surely someone somewhere
sips sherry.

Open Up The Sky

Seriously, the romance of words
surges, a treadle, her social life
like polyester. She knows text,
scripts it in embroidery threads,
works the quilt. The star-
shapes, patience through
winters into spring.
Soft lamps, spectacles.
Hers is textile, paint-in-cloth,
stories whispered. Prism in patches.
Dredged, trundled.
Time backs onto the stitch-
by-stitch, hand-sewn
into second-hand stores
and sold for a dollar.

"It's not fair," she cries
inside, like a child
losing at a deck of cards.
The devil plays with poker
chips while she sits in her rocker
and sucks on the finger of the world.

What does it mean? The quilted sky
answers, reflection on all that comes from
this painted ground.

    The siwash she knit
    while carrying her last.
    She had time then,
    before the bottom fell out
    and she had to work off the farm.

Winter he appeared, a surprise.
She had the one still and laid,
unmarked, along a graveyard path.
Maybe this surprise was for that torture,
so many sweaters and mittens ago.

She bought the maple red,
the black, the smokey white
and knit in hope.
Adding bulk as she grew,
and grew, to her surprise.

I have the siwash now,
for autumn's chill.
A memento to surprises.
And a picture of her in it, 1967.
Ready, as big as she had ever been.

One day I'll return it to the youngest,
to the one who fattened her
through winter, spring and fall,
and stretched the siwash to the limit.

What we hold onto.

A jewel box. Paste pearls,
a broken brooch, a cameo,
brocade, a slip of silk.
A ring, a gold ring, plain, worn.
One set of clip-on earrings,
for good. Her husband's pocket
watch, stopped. What is held:

lace, a cross, coined face of a King.
Prayer beads from wood
still holds the scent of a place
so far away she's lost its name.
Great-great-grandpa was a missionary
there 'til cholera felled him,
bleached his bones under
the Union Jack.
No medals come down this line.

There are some whose nostalgia
is liniment, pungent camphor,
the Tiger Balm of history, while others
give it all up for a peck of memory.
It's a small box without a key.
Open it. Open it. You'll find
a crochet hook size 8,
a pair of brass spectacles
curled under. Here lie journeys
in each calcified stone.
It's all we have, and all we want:
these jewels of accoutrement.
These: a ring, a pearl. A box.

    The hammerhead,
    rock shaped by friction.
    A Mantle rookie card,
    with granny glasses
    in boy's scrawl.
    The Swiss-made watch
    that wintered in a field
    and kept on ticking.

The 'Tex' pellet gun,
birthday number 12,
that nearly took an eye.

The things we keep,
not things really…symbols.
Of what was and is gone.
Of play and fortunes lost.
Of close calls and quality.
Of the loves that formed
and the frictions that burned.

Science says memory locates through
the body entire. Every cell, its nucleus, our atoms.
How holding an object in the palm,
feeling its pulse flow is mystery,
osmotic invisible energy
making meaning. How touch is conduit
to vision. How you can see the thing
but never grasp it. How something so small
is wonderment at what'll hold tomorrow.

Something new to slip through fingers:
a worry doll, a hair clip, something forgotten
and found in a pocket, everything stolen from
a past you only pretend to know and a future
as ellipsis. Holding hard is the belief in this,
a child's first tooth.

When her son was born, a Native friend
took his umbilical and placed it inside
a beaded pouch. Identity, a gift for when

he becomes a man. Soon, too soon.
True, too true. Sometimes she rubs
beads over fingertips and prays
a good prayer
to thank Someone,
Stars Rivers and Light
for all that is held.
All that is held.

His memories of the well,
the fire, the army
are my memories,
passed on in the cells.

I went to Goldsmith's corner,
The Pigeons pub up the road.
There was the well
where they threw his brother,
of which a rebel song was written.
The old stone house the
bastards burned.
The fields out behind
where they scattered
under fire.
All was familiar and near.

In the new country
where his hide was saved,
he hurriedly walked to the
corners of the fields, and
skirted the bluffs, bowed

in thought.
I understood his need to escape.

She is drawn, still, to the rough skin
of houses, to texture, light, touch.
Her dream is to walk past red brick,
fingertips trailing like water on rough edges,
seams of mortar. She dreams
of inhabiting the old home, built to last,
cellar belching out mice, furnace once dedicated
to other fuels now a whisper of heat
on polished wood floors. Home is not home
without hearth, fire, a vase of flowers on the table.

Escape? To be old, to be this woman in this house,
is all the escape she needs. Wiping hands on an apron
is her daily act of grace. In the morning,
she kneels beside the morning glories
on the back fence, weatherbeaten to moonshine.
In the evening, she circumambulates
every direction. In every direction,
something loved is seen.
Someone loved is seen.

Someone loved and loving comes,
over the narrow grid or curve of earth.
A sister, and a nun, from India,
then Pakistan, then Bangladesh,
then Rhodesia, then Ireland,
with curved knives, ritual swords
the brass balancing figures

from another world, the tweed
and tobacco of Donegal.

The folk singers who had seen
the country in painted buses
and returned to sit with you
on make-believe rails,
taught the guts of harmonica,
the heart of the traditionals.
Said you could be someone
and see some things.

The older brothers from their
scattered points on the map,
Victoria one year,
Edmonton the next,
bringing their gifts of love,
shared slang and voice,
adding to the common memory.

It's not enough, just here.
The night is too black
and voices only carry in
a rare air, in uncertain directions.
We need the visits from away
to make away real,
to make our love well-traveled.

There's missing, and waiting, and arriving.
Comings, goings, departures. Anticipating
next time. She's the windvane,
the ancient prow, a masthead, a figurehead,

a siren. She's the maypole, the merry-go-round,
a kite with a merry tail. She's danger, volume,
spin and torque. She's ascendant and descendant,
slip and slide. She's windtunnel, rollercoaster,
a lone figure in that basket in the sky.
She's helium, oxygen, nitrogen, hydrogen,
fertilizer. She's calcium and rain, phosphorus,
aurora, a new-formed constellation.
She's the nebula, she's nuance, she's your dance.
She's energy, synergy, entropy, sympathy,
the beautiful solace of vibration.
She's meteor, mercury, and magic.
She's the harmony in the voice of your air,
life and breath. She's wonder in all
her elements, incantation, oratory.
She's all of that. She's Beauty
holding arms outstretched
to all the four directions,
your sister and your mother
resting till the tarried ships come
sailing home in greeting.

    Arriving on time, arriving late,
    waiting, passing through
    gates, corrals, queues,
    time in confined spaces,
    cubicles, stalls, toilets.
    Waiting to be released,
    to proceed, to ascend.
    Killing, filling time.

Open Up The Sky

The spirit knows no
such confinement as this,
and is off and out into these
distant mountains, skimming
over this ocean, back to the
seas of wheat, and clay cliff-faces
of badlands, inside the
hearts of sisters and brothers
whispering, "Proceed, ascend.
Let's meet near the medicine wheel,
in our prairie valley and sing."

And everywhere is singing.
Sweetgrass woven to a braid, the beat of drums.
Church chorales, not yet museum pieces.
Alleluias and *aves*,
chants, plainsong, the thrum
of her nephew's guitar
as he pretends to be Dylan.
These acts of grace, this music,
the land opened for plough and hearth.
Land and love, opened.

6 a.m. Beijing.
Blue skies,
light dust cover
from Mongolian winds.
Splitting headache
from disturbed sleep
and dust.
A familiar swirl

of dirt smoke
under foot-fall,
like the drought years
walking over summer fallow,
apocalyptic speculation about
the return of dirt drifts
and starvation.
Laden vegetable trucks
on the expressway.
So many mouths to feed.
We belong to the Earth
not it to us.
The land is opened
and thanks is given.

They wanted to be famous.
That was the size of them.
Bigger than Dylan,
as big as the world.
A few learned "Lay Lady, Lay"
and "Blowing in the Wind"
and shared the Word of Bob
in village pubs and homecomings
with varying degrees of appreciation,
expecting one day to be the next Bob.

You learn, in time,
to sing for small worlds,
for this few here,
these friends and lovers
in small and significant worlds,
where love has opened
and the ground is familiar.

Open Up The Sky

If you leave home enough, travel far as they did,
farther, if you leave you come back to the same place.
It's not the spirit leaving. Home isn't left for memory,
it's carried in a handbag filled with all the places
you will never be, and still is home.
The spirit's singing songs the old abandon,
the young set to a different beat, but keep the tune.
There's more drum to it but the melody is there,
haunting dreams, perfection in a rear-view mirage.
There's only forward where they all reside,
large, small, the ones you pick up and swing
with the glory of it all, young loved faces
and older graces, these willow ones
bringing wild roses and the sweet smell of pine.
Love is astringent, survives dust bowls,
dust heaps, the deluge of water to send
a small bloom anywhere you go.
You love, and there you are.

    There you are among the toppled
    pioneer shacks, returning to earth.
    One hundred years of history, born yesterday,
    made of wood, mud and necessity.

    Beyond the aspen and poplar
    the rock is the oldest rock,
    meteoric, made of exploding stars
    and the drift of the continents.
    The Forbidden City, Newgrange on the Boyne,
    the bones of the badlands,

arrowheads, bayonets, iron wheel.
All born yesterday next to the worn
and buckled mountains of the uplands.

You are there, walking over and through,
young, too young to feel your age
and to know the ground under foot.

There you are on the waterways,
craft on a river, upstream, down,
currents, rapids, horsepower on a lake.
Some prefer whitewater, a squall,
zipping up when mosquitoes are thick.
Others chase a quiet solitude,
fishing line cast at the extremes
of day and evening. Your heart is a bobbin,
gauging depths and shallows as though
measurement gave answers. Reel in.
Kindle a fire at the next lea.
Find metamorphic, sedimentary,
turn a fossil in your hand.
Legacy is bone, yes,
the sound of water on rock,
and it is this, too:
a short century traded for
millennia written on shale,
the gravitas of stone,
hope in a paddle, a ripple,
the hunger of love in water.
Reel it in. Reel.

Open Up The Sky

You are there on the river's cliff
a tumbling game down the soft sand
to the water's edge.
Gunshot in a free tumble was the game.
Someone is fishing from the rocks
for jack and whitefish, and the ferry
is weighed down with lake people,
heading up to Big and Little Bear,
and farther into the shield to the
dead cold waters, to uranium and nickel
country, where the dog islands were,
where you were swarmed by the hungry
ones as a kid and shit your pants
getting up a good climbing tree.
A man named Knutson threw the
sled dogs a sucker and called
off the pack.
From then, you were not one of the island people
nor one of the black lakers.
The open plains, the sandy cliff,
somewhere to tumble, somewhere you
could see the dogs coming.

You are never so much yourself
as when you are going somewhere.
Doing something, anything.
Reading a good book under a
spring tree humming with bees,
yes, and later the open road,
first dusty, then highway,
wide open. You remember
summer with a small baby,

an old car, no air, going to Alberta.
You didn't know
he could drink a bottle
of Coke so fast, sweat beaded
under that hot sun quicker than
a gopher finds his hole.
Nothing better, then, than
jumping in a lake.
Clear lakes, salt lakes,
open road, dinosaur bones,
nothing on the radio.
Nothing, everything
around you an oven,
thunderclouds gathering.
Heat, and the open road.
A destination.
This is park, this is drive.
This shift of gears, open.

    Sit here, where the world stops.
    Fine bone China, fake coffee,
    the smell of dust.

    He sees through cracks
    in a bamboo wall to remote
    valleys he knows.
    By this time of spring
    grasses are tall
    enough to sway.
    A solitary monk or poet
    ponderous on a distant
    height of land.

Open Up The Sky

Here, machines carve
the silt and sand,
reroute the river's flow,
and footpaths are paved.
There, slow rivers still
cut and shape young valleys.
Lone walkers keep paths barely worn.

Sit here, under the inflatable red arch
between how people lived and how they will live.
Your kingdom for the battered tin
canteen of childhood, hiking quarter to quarter
in search of a bin town with well and livery.

Room is being cleared for the future.
Open sewers and coke burning fires
had their day.
Now is petroleum's time,
television's time,
prosperity's time,
double time's time.

Sit here in the dust and smog, and go there.
Take a drink from your dented
army canteen, around a campfire
on a creek bed.
Nothing clogging the nostrils.
Hum of bees, trickle of stream
over a beaver dam.

Birds have, it seems, an instinct, fly long distances,
return to that same spot they've lighted.

They come for landing, silent or give voice
to one another that here, this place, remembers
there, that one, and glad at this safe harbour.
They search a corner for mementoes left behind
in feathers, watch sky for signs of danger,
nest, roost, make sense of tall grasses.
Their work is perfect, hatched fragility
to transience, the hope of fossils.
They pull the sky together, dart through clouds,
inhabit spirit space where light and sound
provide a show, a shining truth, now.
They symbolize much and are so little,
for the most part, sometime creatures you
hold in palm of hand, or watch aloft,
bow heads at their great wingsweep, circling.

I don't know why I think of birds when you are flying
or wings when you are east and I am west,
but someway they are proof:
unto home we all return.

    Strange, artful birds, at new heights.
    Days on sacred ground we smile,
    listen, go within more than on days
    of utility.
    The haze, blossoms, sweat in
    the air, the trampled stone under
    foot, are rarefied by the tremble of
    awe and humility's silence.
    Enzymes that flood the veins
    with reverence work overtime
    on these grounds.

Open Up The Sky

That explains the absence of
violence, the longing to
speak foreign tongues, the
exchange of wordless eye messages
of respect, even love.
The potent particulates
in the air explain why birds
are more self assured,
fly with less utility, more art.

Watching starlings and flycatchers in
these mountains, I think of the
curious magpie of Batoche,
the darting swallows of Fort San.
There is a feeling of home,
a world away from home.

In my heart, hummingbirds.
They are REM sleep of the world,
our dreams written on wings small
as eyelids. What is seen,
if you are such a tiny bird?
What tasted? Sounded? How to find
a nest laid in the beating thrum
of a large world?

The world made smaller:
today I watched tiny people,
China's *Cirque de Soleil*
dance Swan Lake.
Hummingbird people.
Motions of grace.

Everywhere, body and soul,
flight, and movements
toward heavens.

Hummingbirds.

    A shift, a shuffle.
    A cloud opens, cuts a light stream
    over land.
    Awakenings.
    Appearances.
    Voices carry across the lake.
    A paddle's droplets drum
    on taut skin. Someone shouts
    in hope of an echo.
    There is no telling what or who
    is stirred, but it is much and many.
    The ripple and wave of water
    repeats in forest and hill
    and out into the peopled places.

    There is a single wave, a cut of light,
    a solo shout that sounds out into one
    small world.

    The hummingbird.
    The bee-bird.
    Somewhere along the line
    wires got crossed.
    A head-on collision of insect
    and bird during a tectonic shift
    or meteor strike.

Open Up The Sky

Another in a long line
of evolutionary screw-ups,
perfect in their imperfection.

She watches them hover at the
sugar water and is thankful
creation abounds in happy
accidents.
What of selfish man, violent man?
A species of shark flopped on
volcanic lands, knocked up
by a vulture.
Her hummingbirds open
up so many possibilities.

Some people call it accident.
Some prefer serendipity.
She calls it purposefulness,
the random grace of chaos.
Yes, there are griefs:
a fawn at the side
of the long road
between Greenwood
and Osoyoos, where heat
rises over border water.
Like a child born cleft,
or a spill of berries picked
all day long. All day,
she sees this hardened world,
waits for rightness,
a change in the weather.
She watches steam over orchards,

a spider web longer than a field
which clings to nothing,
or at least something she can't see.
Rain, and sun, and rain again,
the comic antics of grouse.
It's laughter, this magic,
this day by day rising, greeting,
wondering for a next radical
inversion. Is God to blame
for caprice, or do we play this game
without recourse to patience?
Evolution changes all of it,
and we are none the wiser.
Mystery is ether, and paradox
is either, and neither.
She remembers, casts a line,
skips stones and blesses
ripples spinning.

    This variety is perfection, so it's said.
    How odd, this, how odd.
    How strange, how strange.
    He stands just shy of embracing
    his own oddity and that of the world.

    Why this eye for delicate and usual,
    for frightened and abandoned?

    The warmer things,
    the non-judging things,
    he studies bewildered, awed.

Open Up The Sky

A fawn, yes, in the iris bog.
A baby porcupine quivering on a branch.
Turtles too slow to beat traffic,
now claw and tail artifacts in his
glove box.
But people…there's something
too strange, too mysterious.

There is a nature not of this odd place
that absorbs with a transient's attention.
Just passing through.
Just passing through.

In the darkness, solitude opens.
A thick skein unravels into oneness.
Connection; all connects in the movement:
bow, exult, bless.
We see differently, then.
In these moments, touch is not enough,
may shatter delicate film on a butterfly
wing, can sting. It's like tracing air
over etchings: translucence that tells
each story. Honeycomb, spider web,
fine structure of bones in the wrist,
the turn of a pen.
Messages inscribe on this skin
of the birthing world, kindle hope,
ignite, bring every breath back.
The womb, the round belly,
this chrysalis, open.

The womb,
the round belly.
Naked on a quilt
covered floor,
resting her back,
curtains closed to
summer's dry heat.
I traced with a hand
the hot air from her,
a warm mountain
soon to erupt.

We think it's mystery. Part the mists
with eyes of love and all is plain.

These plains, too, open.
They lead in all directions:
sea ice, mountains west, valleys east,
and surely south where ghosts have names
the world will recognize.
No one makes a last stand:
everywhere, the earth is bone.
Our stories carried with us in every
palm, in each wound and wonderment.
Summer's heat and winter cold, too,
open to each other, part the veils
which shade our vision from
the other worlds.
Stand still; turn in a circle;
they are right here.
Eruption is an exclamation
point on the essay of the world,

and happens every season.
Sometimes, as she says,
we are simply present and we see it.

Spirit is a funnel.
Spirit is a colander sifting sand to glass
where lightning strikes.
Spirit is an ember, crushed ice when
she's in labour.

Birth, death, prairie, ocean:
the maelstrom is within us,
love, our key for entry.

    The back of the hand.
    Mountain, valley, river, desert.
    Trace elements of old wounds,
    scarred, badly healed.
    Spotted from impacts of
    wind, fire, ice, acid, stone.
    Cold aches, age aches,
    the aches of labour.

    So much shovel work.
    Mountains of gravel on
    the desolate Alberta rails.
    Mountains of wheat on flats.
    Mountains of top soil
    turned for grain and garden.
    Mountains of red earth
    for the final plantings

of family, friend, neighbour,
in frozen ground, mud and dust.

The crevices of knuckle.
The whited burn of thumb.
The pocks between arteries.
The scabs at the joints.
The random cuts on fingers.
Stories written and told
on the back of the hand.

Stretch marks, pock marks, the creaky joints
of history. What's bred in the bone,
carried in flesh. She says,
"My stretch marks are highways;
see how I've grown." Hands on bellies
feel movement, a finger traces soft rivers in skin.
Silver and purple, badges of life borne
and brought to bear. The skin and bone
of the world, its flesh and heart, blood.
Earth, wood, wind and water conspire.

I wonder about the invisible.
Are people like cilia? Without these,
we can't breathe, atoms and dust
cleared through deep breath
of meditation. Each life part of the whole,
every cell. Is a person metonymy?
Or is it in trees and their absence,
the clear-cut scar waiting for planting?
Once, were the plains full of otherness?
How do deserts grow, hills form?

Open Up The Sky

What are badlands, and why do we name them
without metaphors for what they may be,
the weathered scar of history?

Here, another sunrise. Highway noise travels.
Just over there, lavender christens
morning's gold with purples.

    I wonder about people,
    how they scatter and breathe,
    continue, invisible to me.
    I recall a name once intimate
    and the troubles she had.
    I remember laughter on old sofas,
    pictures taken with a boy picking
    his feet, and that boy is now off
    in China, with a curious baby
    wobbly yet on her legs.
    Where is Jeff, his mad laugh,
    his bent humour, his lust, his anger?
    Has he made it through?
    People move in and out of view.
    New mechanisms of connection
    are the gauze that puts form
    to invisiblity. Those we search
    for are found, somewhere,
    at home, at love, in deep life.
    He is out there somewhere,
    floating, like the rest of us,
    scattered, breathing, continuing.

The friends we've lost, and those we've found.
A baby picture and that same child, two decades later,
expression on her sweet face undisturbed.
A sudden reminder of someone we'd thought
lost to time, or pain,
an old hurt chilling through a phantom scar,
or remembered delight through a slip of music.

They say the brain remembers only
emotion up to brimming:
love, passion, anger, shame, grief.
These we remember, we know, we feel.
Feel. All others:
passing through.

Sometimes, though, a surprise.
Acquaintance changes, deepens,
finds a different spot inside a heart
you thought already full. Somehow
you expand, fill up with yet another soul
you call a friend. How strange,
gifted once again with such expansion,
and room for more. Room for more,
this road, the remembered breath
taken in as deep as anyone you've
tried to forget. You can try:
there's always room,
for more.

    He is a bush man, my friend,
    prone to frantic isolation within his brain.
    I am a man of the fields,

claustrophobic in lake land,
prone to frantic isolation within his brain.
Get him out on the water
and he's a fast talker.
You can't keep up with
his mouth and better not try.
The valve is open, and his pent
up Buddhist steam escapes.
There is nothing.
We are all one thing.
What minor importance, our lives.
The earth will be fine without us.
Each of these thoughts,
a stream of consciousness volume
that lasts all afternoon and well
into the evening and next day.
I let him know what he knows,
and listen in hope of his influence.
His volumes now condensed
within me, in space made available
by love.

Cycles expand and contract:
Today I watched children play in sand,
a beach, sails on water, birds.
Not my children, not my blood,
but friends who greet with hugs.
A small boy places his hand in mine, a trust.
The baby girl cuddles into my breast.
There is laughter, sun, wind.
What will be their story? A picnic,
a day on the beach with a friend.

In time, they will forget my face,
even these small bodies they
now live in. They too, will grow,
and hold their own.
I feel time in a single cell,
in a small hand around
my smallest finger.
We walk on sand.
Forgotten joys bubble
into geysers. Jeffrey says,
"Look!" and opens kisses
on his sister.
This too shall pass.
This, too, shall return.
Picnic, sail, this love by water.

    He is a runner.
    And I walk
    on the beach,
    the wave's drift and deposit.
    From the height of a dune
    I see him vanish
    around a bend where
    surf and rock spit merge.
    He will go as long as there is
    running ground, and never far enough.

    Big water silences me,
    stops me in my tracks.
    A bird's skeleton.
    The trail of a tailed thing.

Open Up The Sky

A furry man frying sausage,
holding in a beach stomach.
Everything in its place.

He never stops.
He burns up his waking hours,
keeps himself lean, hungry.
Like me, there is somewhere
he needs to get, undefined, illusive.
He gulps air.
I sip.
He hurries.
I slow.
The singlular rhythm of the waves
drives us both.

For her, life has slowed to a walk.
Meditation comes slowly.
Her entertainment is found
in the families of quail
which bound and abound.
She never tires of their bobbing
headgear, knows they're ungainly.
She stops to smell flowers,
asks their names. Roses
in abundance, and peonies,
phlox, lupins, irises just ending,
and more, never seen before.
Tiny magical stems and blooms,
nestled in underbrush. She chats
with an elderly gardener

around the corner: two decades
of love in soil. "I just can't
keep up with the weeds!"
Laughter. "I'll leave them
for my children."
Children speed by on tricycles.
Three teenagers run by.
She greets them, walks along
to the music on her iPod.
Debussy, Claire de Lune.
Holy, holy. All warms,
a blanket of holy.
In the west, behind the hills,
setting sun, still shadows
on the quiet lake. A sail, a laugh.
She likes even pavement,
the slow move into
a summer breeze.
Shapes of things to come.

    One slow walker can throw
    the whole world off.
    They laugh.
    "I don't know if he is
    thoughtful or thoughtless."
    They idle as the walker crosses,
    in sandaled feet.
    Not dazed, but nearly.
    Not contemplative, but possibly.
    Not deliberate, but maybe.
    He is too slow to follow,
    too slow to have a destination.

Open Up The Sky

    For thirty seconds, their world
    stops and they remark on
    the phenomenon of slow
    and how rare its appearance.

The world is there. Interior,
a space of images. Words emerge,
never quite right yet exact.
She hears a self speak inside,
opens her mouth. Gibberish,
perhaps another language
borrowed from a planet.
Closer than blood, closer than
the nearest constellation.
There's exploration. She navigates
internal rivers, breathes under
water. Sometimes, she enters
dreams, but the inevitable occurs:
she wakes up. Breath is slow
until the rush, until the rush.
The mirror fogs. Still, she can
see someone shapely there,
memory. A girl riding a bicycle
along Temperance Street,
silver buildings in the distance
the mirage she chases.
Across the river, the Mendel
winks a joke and Spadina
winds to a future she may
never realize. She wheels
to a glimmer of shining bridges.
Return is her silver feather

of hope, and tells a story:
osmosis like a wind chime.
A ringing of bells. Bells, ringing.

A whirling cloud
seeming from another world
spins over Diefenbaker Park,
right above the train bridge.
Traffic stops on Spadina West.
This could be something.

A stroll involving kisses,
prone in grasses along
a lilac thicket.
A day at the flats,
through which strange
weather gathered.
Provoking rash,
natural disaster decisions,
such as chasing twister clouds
and kissing, prone.

They stand and watch it hover,
nerves of light ripping through
its dirty grey-green shell
exploding thunder nearly instant,
threatening to grow a tail.
Some run from spectacle
but many gather, locked in
embrace, fresh kisses and
gibberish on their lips
as the alien cloud breaks

and weeps dirty tears,
rinsing the newly intimate.

The same river bank watches a man cry.
She wishes she could say different,
some comfort for this death of what they thought was love.
Deep kisses not enough. She knows his tongue
more than expected, waits for
something more than this could ever be.
She remembers a willow tree, apt, above
them. Hands entwined, she whispers
"Sorry". What else? Courage comes from
kisses past and future, from the sweet taste
of somebody else, some other time,
expectancy speaking in tongues.
Hers is the glossalia of trust:
this can and will be better.
Someone else, some other time.
After the weeping, the season still
will shift, the river alter course.
She does not claim to know,
as yet, the kiss she will remember
all her life. Diefenbaker Park,
a summer night to come.
Later, they watch their
child dancing on the same green
where she remembers kisses.
She spreads her arms to the summer world,
to all holiness east of rivers
where water speaks in tongues.

Graphite water under the train bridge,
film of deadfall, foam and scum.
So many loves cut footpaths on these banks,
some overgrown, others kept well-worn.

I left a notebook on a rock,
and went to clamber up the bank.
In it drawings, words, and a picture
of a woman who said she loved me.
A keepsake from a lust gone bad.
A snapshot of a longing extinquished.

I returned to find it missing,
and scoured the shore,
not for drawings or words,
but for the picture,
which I prayed had not
gone the way of deadfall, foam
and scum.
And with darkness came stars
reflected in the black water,
some of them extinct,
like these loves
thought to be eternal.

What I wonder is when
love became the only reason.

Then, it was an order on a menu
for a peasant wife. If you were
lucky, she was pleasant, maybe pretty.
Somewhere began a dance,

Open Up The Sky

the plough became a fiddle,
the girl more than hands for making
families. Somewhere became
soft whispers, a caress stolen
under a harvest moon. Then time
turned and suddenly,
a cameo brooch became an old charade.
A woman's story, or a man's, the same.

Denim is all-season wear.
You can still string clothes along a line,
turn a wheel with pins between your lips
and call it love. You can bury your
face in the dry cotton pinwheel of love,
and photograph a fiction.
Tumbleweed is a woman rolling
over grace, reclaiming space.
A combine is a place where
a voice on the radio sings of all these:
where we've been.
A picture or a tune, anthems claiming
love is yours, and mine.

Fifty-eight years and he no longer knows her.
She could be his patient mother
or the long walker from up the corner,
a sweetheart of his phantom memory.
Whoever she is, he smiles
when she comes to visit,
and wants the tone of love
her voice holds,
a tone that left long ago,

but returns now that he is
a child again and has lost his rage.

Love was always the reason.
Just there, available, like salt or air.
Felt, absorbed. A God thing, given,
infused. Running through the dry
and the wet, tumbling and whispering,
beyond property, free for the asking.
Withheld, nothing lives.
Not weed, not lips, not dance, not moon.

If these are truths, there must be courage.
Courage to ask, to expect, to believe, to hope.
Where does courage come from?
All elements lend it whispers,
Sinew and bone tell its story,
liquid wet of wishing, blood as water.
After these and before them,
the asking. An outstretched hand:
child, lover, friend, mother,
slippery as you climb one more bluff,
lift feet over another dune.
They say the prairie's flat:
I say that if you walk it, the ground's
uneven. Pot holes, gopher holes,
an abandoned well. Boulders become
rocks becomes stones become sand,
and still the prairie holds her hand
to courage, to the reaching hope
of a soul who says, "Please,
please," in every language.

Open Up The Sky

Wind and water answer
in a poem, in softer sounds
of invitation. Love is bred
in place of chimera, the touchstone
of alone, captured.
Courage whistles, love answers,
knowledge for the asking.

Punnichy to Saskatoon,
ninety miles per hour
in a government car.
He has retrieved a run away
who didn't want to be retrieved.
The sooner he gets her to the
group home, the sooner his fright
can rest. Would she jump at that
speed? Not likely. Could she be so
desperate, so courageous?
She's just a kid, but gutsy enough to
hitch from Saskatoon to Punnichy.
She scares him.

Is there courage in this?
Transporting runaways
turned over by the police,
who fed them sandwiches and
milk until the transporter
arrived.
A girl as mute as these
scab lands that are a blur
to her teary eyes as she stares

out the window.
Lands her people got pushed
into by sweepers and takers.

"I hope you had some fun, at least."
He finally breaks the silence.
That took courage.
"Some," she said.
That, too, took courage.

Drifting from land to sky.
A question of belonging.
Terrestrial. Empyreal.
And back again, in cycle.

There is a current there,
dry but glacier laced,
scented crocus and sage,
hide and hair, bone and flint.
Metis fiddle rides it, faint.
Skin drum rides it, faint.
The twang of barbed wire.
The rip and roar of rifle fire.
Uranium dust, diamond dust,
Diesel, dung and turned earth.

A heaven is held in an image,
in memory turned, shaped, distilled.
The uplifting detail,
The drifting from ground to sky,
Must be.
Must be.

Open Up The Sky

It's in the question,
"What is it you really want?"
as if this could be answered.
As if there were options.
Answers may lie in the open road,
or a closed one. Barriers
and flashing lights at a night-
time skid where something ended.

As if courage is anything other
than wanting to ask. If it is true,
that it shall be given, then the question
remains: "What's the gift?"
The given, the received.

We watch them: yard sale junkies,
a hitchhiker going west, south,
anywhere his thumb can take him.
The farmer fencing, fending off
mule deer and miseries,
a garden terminated at a snail's pace.
Slugs, dust, the born-again hope
of a shelter belt in bloom.
Wild roses and the scent of longing,
the taste of hops. Everything held
in a seed. Everyone held in a circle.

The question whispers in scrub-land,
in river-land: "What is it you really need?
Is anything more than right here? Here?"

Distant, a silhouette: could be a tree,
could be a man. Above, a flashing light.
A flash, and light.

Sometimes, it must happen,
that from this height of land
a man is seen walking in the
depths of the basin,
his life on his back.
Down from Val Marie or Mankota,
skirting Breed Creek in search of answers,
and the new buffalo.

This is not Banff, not the Bruce,
or Prince Albert.
People sightings are rare here,
as rare as the bald eagle or
black bear elsewhere.
Conversation is with the self.
The only music blaring
is the beat of sage grouse wings,
the crackle of withering grass,
a howling wind section.

This scar land, where you go to hide,
where no one wants to come and find you.
Black and gray, on black and gray,
skewed perspectives, tough to capture
with gouache and pencil.

Something catastrophic happened here.
A thousand year incident involving sun and ice.
God in long-time scooped a hollow
and left it for the antelope and heat.

Is that a man out there or a tree,
wavered by sun, clinging to life?
What does either want or need?

Open Up The Sky

Water and light.
Water and light.

It's that particular type of drowning.
You are born from water before you learn to breathe,
and it's the element of return. Sometimes,
water is salt: oceans, seas,
the remnant inland lake
at Manitou Beach. There,
you cannot sink,
can almost walk on miracles.
There, your whole body is open to light,
and the moon casts beacons, waves
on sun-kissed skin
to teach you how to listen.
When water fills your ears, and light your eyes,
language dissolves to pulse: you become
glacier, journey, molecule.
There is no other kind of music.

Such a strong swimmer,
so afraid of drowning.
Maybe he had a rough ride
in the womb.
Joggled in swerving and overturned cars,
shaken when blows were avoided or
night escapes on foot made necessary.

It's said the womb is secure.

Once off a dock, Denare Beach,
before he became a dolphin,
he went under for the count.
A pretty girl he was trying to impress
with a dive in deep water.
A girl will remove
your fear of drowning,
your fear of heights,
your fear of intimacy.

Over his head and sinking fast,
he thought to become weightless,
drop to the bottom and push
himself up.
But his air left before bottom came.

Looking up, a flash of green bikini.
A bigger girl took the plunge,
hauled him up around his thin tummy.
Did his sweetheart come then and
kiss the breath back into him?
No. And so he learned to swim.

Under water, light is honeycomb on tile
unless you're lucky enough to inhabit a lake,
or a sea spidery with shapes. They're different,
as you've found, these waters. One soft,
even when it's hard, with muddy ochres,
sometimes leeches, once a snake
when she was a child and learned to fear.
The other aqua, a tourist postcard,
stingray alley in Belize where fish are kittens

Open Up The Sky

nipping at heels. Like anywhere,
we throw them scraps,
entice them from a shelf
of purple corals fanning themselves
in the lucid world. Sometimes she makes
angels, preferring this place to snow.
Today she was a large bird, arms become wings,
eyes closed to let the filigreed pretense
pierce irises black and deep, buoyant.
Nothing reaches bottom.
Nothing's heavy in a realm of light.
Liquid is magic, and if we do
pass this way again, she'd wish for
fins and gills, depth, and the ability to sink.

He has a little breath now.
Or maybe it is taken away
by thoughts of depths.
So many deeps and bottoms
he wishes to explore.

Treasures under falls and rapids.
Submarine surfaces silvered with light.
Great steamers capsized by a weight
of horses, stores and adventurers.
Priestly trinkets in French River torrents,
copper pot, crucifix, hatchet.
The currencies of conversion.

He is a surface diver, a long swimmer.
Like his father, who crossed rivers
in pursuit of drifting beach balls.

On the surface, where those on shore
could admire his flippers and fins.

He used to breathe water but now,
when the impulse to go deep comes,
he feels the limits of his breath,
chokes and surfaces.
Going deep is another instinct
entirely. It is there, somewhere
at the bottom.

The bridal veil in Kagawong.
Behind its thin, silver curtain
a slick clay wall gouged
from the bed of an extinct sea.

God's home. God's drink of water.

Here are things you had never seen.
Not on the plains, not in bush country.
Badland's carnage was long reduced
to bone, but here a different kind
of pulse and impulse.

This is where the salmon end
their suicide struggle,
where the white bellies flash
and corpses bleach in impossible
shallows.
This is where spectacle makes
you weep autumn after autumn.
Where fossil foot stones remind you
of island age and life's brevity.

Open Up The Sky

Down every back road
another total life,
in so much detail.
The junk collector's
apparent chaos.
The immaculate tillers,
with no stray blossom.
The self-sustainers off the grid,
letting things go back to wild.
Horse people with their courses.
God people with their crosses.

It's too much for me, the intricacies.
Too much in the open and behind doors.
Except from above,
where the patterns unfold
in field patches and yard patches.
Where a jagged plow furrow merges
with circular and straight in artful
harmony.
Where rust, soot and salt
are a stitch or stroke.
Where trimmed and untrimmed
belong, and every back road
a connecting thread.

How many eternities make her weep?
Prayers for women gone too soon,
visions accompanying them
to invisible gardens.
Tenderness: friends with offerings,

a Persian artist who holds her,
serves tea, cardamom, cream
and honeysuckle. Two sprigs
in a room: this is heaven.
She receives a chador vibrant
with history and remembers lineage,
cloth speaking holy names.
The only water on this night:
salt tears, more than joy and sorrow.
More departures, more fingerlings
reaching, stroking
the skin beneath her skin.
For an atom's breath, she lost
thought to a brief breeze,
and scented attars opened
portals into love. The weeping
is for grace. A happenstance,
and she imbibes grace,
feasts on mercy and renewal.

    Just to have a brief breeze
    snatch up thought
    and hang it on a good limb
    to air and spring.

    He sees an extraction
    that none are willing to make.
    "You can't be squeamish
    with a thing like that,"
    the old man said. "Give
    me the pliers."

Open Up The Sky

This is the same neighbour
who knew a good back
hammering would dislodge
the pretzel that turns a boy blue.
Now, a honeysuckle twig
driven three inches up the
jaw line, and here he is
again with his barnyard first-aid.

"You leave the damn thing
and it'll be sprouting leaves
by morning."
The others avert their eyes
as, in one swift yank,
the sapling is uprooted.

What had been forgotten: the colour of water
in sloughs, inexplicable puddles teeming with birds.
In the mountains, liquid silver green above Banff.
A contented moose grazes the south side of the road.
A doe crosses tarmac, not a care in the world,
oblivious to chaos and tourists. Later, mule deer
west of Alsask, a dip in the road past Kindersley.

An ironic, self-conscious smile, getting teary:
the Saskatchewan
border, glances off road to elevator sentinels
left standing. Some buildings are derelict
but the land is there, the endless seagreen land.
Yellow begins to bloom. Sun is there,
and sky as far as she can see.
She knows where she's going.

Heather Cardin and Rob O'Flanagan

She knows where. Rosetown, Harris,
Delisle. Steel and rails, a slim bird sailing.
She knows. She's going.

Smuts to Alvena to Wakaw.
Yellow Creek to Meskanaw to home.
Familiar towns, tiny, tree-lined islands
in long grasses and patchwork fields.

There are rolling hills out that way,
and the valleys of extinct rivers.
Some old Indian history is still
turned up in cultivator blades.
But the attractive forces are in
opposite directions.

The wind owns two of them now.
The graveyards have grown and
deer far outnumber children.
Clothes pegs have grayed on brittle lines
and the trap-lines are long abandoned.
Committees of the old keep
church paint freshened,
until outpaced by the sun.
Homes turn to four fading walls
and plywood blinds shop interiors.

There is talk of a boom in the papers,
but not in these long suffering towns,
which have seen their young drift to
cities, to oil patches and sands,
in the currents money makes.

Open Up The Sky

The old have become too old
to keep house and home.

Home to Meskanaw to Yellow Creek.
Wakaw to Alvena to Smuts,
then off in all scattered directions.

Cities still turn suddenly. No eternal suburbs
lit by smog horizons, exits that really depart.
Suddenly you're in beaver country
picking your way through saskatoon bushes
about to burgeon. Suddenly Wilf and Rita
are at the door, quiet smile and giggle
you'd know anywhere. The traffic
on 14th Street is constant,
somehow reassuring, moves east and west.
North and south are streets across a river.
Every time you cross it, exclamations
and remembrances. Growth, yes,
but you are still in your element.
Around every corner lies a story.
You like it. You like this,
have come full circle.

Unsettled again,
I sit among my boxed things
and imagine a fire pit
in the dunes of Carter's Bay,
the dunes of Cranberry Flats,
the dunes of the Great Sand Hills.

There is always a place for a small fire,
always some gathered deadfall to stoke it,
something fragrant to scent the flames.

Alone or with madly dancing friends,
a fire captures me, takes me inside,
long enough to find my place again.

Another evening of memories.
Reminiscence circles: his grey hair,
her change from early plumage.
Statements are questions,
the rising inflection at the end,
segues to "I'm not sure"
from the certainties of youth.
We discuss Lawren Harris,
the cost of frames, the price of fame,
children. His son is Vietnamese,
their daughter from China.
This is a prairie city of rivers,
of Superstore and corner confectionery,
summer cruises down 8th Street.
Some things never change.
Places fragment into our mind's eyes
as we wrap ourselves in velveteen
stories of once upon a time.
Here we are. Here we are.

In places where painters go,
we smoked and talked,
friends and I.

Open Up The Sky

A. Y. Jackson sat above those falls,
rolled his own, scanned bough
and rapid for the force.
We all carved our signatures
in the lookout's rail and bowed
to the old pulse there.

High above Grace Lake,
Frank Carmichael's church,
Paul and I with cameras
and strong cigarettes,
at the height of turkey vultures,
on worn mountains, hot to touch,
the hermetic painter's hooded form
still hunched there over island sketches,
quavering with the old pulse.

And out in Greg Hardy country,
Jon and I on silent walks. I smoke
rolled Drum tobacco, inhale his sadness.
Up subtle rises, along deer path,
dirt road and stubble field.
The light plucking of wind over wheat,
a mountain of vapor rising
where the creek cuts silver to
the river, and the last of day
sets the west on fire.
And the old pulse flows
through us, bowed, silent.

The city talks. All night long, traffic pulses
and a streetlight shines in the summer walls.

A friend discusses and dismisses Bateman.
I visit studios full of pottery and paintings.
Sal says the older she gets the more she needs beauty.
Amen, and amen. She works clay,
makes orchids from Saskatchewan's soil,
while I carry it between my toes after the river,
scramble on all fours up dunes.
The current rises, the current rushes.
On the dining table, three white peonies bow
heads in different directions.
The scent of diesel and woodsmoke.
Steak and fish on the grill. Saskatoon pie.
Three children climb on my back at Riverside pool.
I am surrounded. The First Nations return
and claim this water. My sister executes
two perfect dives and a back flip.
We all applaud in the deep end.
The world applauds sound, sight,
the scents of the city.
This breath fills every longing as
I wait for the next hot kiss.
The now, and the heat. The heat.

The city cries and babbles on.
A constant din cloaked in smog.
The eyes blink and turn frenetic.
Over-stimulated, your force
is thrown, spent, into the
flow.

Queen and Spadina.
The river of humanity rises and rushes.

Open Up The Sky

You hear five languages merge
at a crosswalk pause.
A late Eritrean breakfast on Bloor
where a desert movie plays.
And you know there is much
you have yet to see.

Some currents take you
into skies, others into streets.
You tell yourself, as you float,
that you are singular in the drift,
but it pulls you in and along,
sometimes beautifully, against
your will.

Beautifully, against your will,
you go with the carnival's flow.
The rides haven't changed
since those elevated summers
when the six hundred pound man
orchestrated thrill rides
and freak shows from the
seat of a customized golf cart.
And the carnies with their
burned out voices
and snake oil pitches,
they are just the same.
Selling off chances at
a marksman's eye
and big leaguer's arm,
off chances at high focus,
as you aim for the giant
teddy, and attain the rabbit's
foot as a consolation prize.

With all of it, wonderment. A sense of purpose,
whys and wherefores, the thought of how
magic is mystery only as novelty. A hat trick,
a guitar trick, waiting for the light to change trick.
At a cafe, you photograph tattoos on a muscular
New Zealander while he chats up a beauty
in dreadlocks. Originally from Rosetown,
she studied French when she was a child,
and your sister, her teacher, recognizes her.
Small world at Five Corners, the convergence
of lives, music till the skies decide.
After ozone, the scent of coffee, a slice of dusk.
After dark, Pam makes tea and wonderment:
is this the way it is? Would time lead you out,
hold your visitor's hand, the air remain
static? A bike backfires,
residual fireworks bring you to focus.
Your skin is an oil-stained rainbow on a window
of pavement, and Garry plays guitar, singing
to the wild wild world.

A biker chick captured
on a 20th Street intersection,
flashing a breast from the back
of a beat up black Harley.
A kind of, "Here kid, let's make this last."
He fumbled for the focus ring,
a shaky finger found the shutter,
and he mouthed, "Thank you,
thank you, thank you."

Open Up The Sky

Wandering Saskatoon with a Nikon,
paid for with the emergency money
his father sent, telling himself it was
worth every penny, and that some
magic would save him from the street,
as he couch surfed
and tried to find his own eyes.

Sometimes, even now, he indulges
in the dream that one day he
will be found and named the next
Henri Cartier-Bresson, or at the least,
see with his own eyes, and shoot with
a steady hand.

Honey, that biker chick was at Value Village today.
Aged a bit, cut her hair short, a few more piercings.
Her 'n her man buying leather jackets.
In summer, I could see the inks above one breast,
both biceps. He slammed money down,
punctuation I kinda liked.
They walked past me 'n four women speaking Cree.
I was waiting for mother. She moves slow
these days hauling the oxygen tank.
It's on wheels, anyways. The lady next to me
narrated their long drive from Pelican Narrows.
(I once wrote a poem about
that place for a contest needing
that particular name. Pelican.)
Then rain came. And then the rain,
and the poem that is
Circle Drive North to family,

Dad spittin' cherry pits in a wooden bowl,
Ange's wildflowers in a metal vase
from the VV boutique, $1.99,
to Kim's explanation of the end of the world
as we know it. Here, now.
The end of this world, as we know it,
and couldn't come better. I'm ready.
If this is all there is? Just fine with me. Just fine.

Today, I watched the clouds for horsemen,
and saw a stallion's head
where others see a rabbit,
or a woman on a motorcycle,
a mane of hair kicked up in the wind.

The Incredible String Band Garry sent
was playing on the car stereo,
a mystic fervor from another time,
when Jesus was a pop star.
When clouds held such promise,
and the end seemed near.

We felt safe out there on the
sparse plains, where nothing
particularly strategic stood.
Until we learned our big skies
were the intercept zones
and mushroom clouds would rain
irradiated fire on our heads.

So much talk of how and when
the world would end.

Open Up The Sky

Violent and retributive scenarios
of collapse, meltdown, evaporation.
Some zealots built bunkers,
some laid up stores in basements,
now rusty and wormy, no longer replenished.

Something will end the world as we know it,
not a sudden flash, but a long, slow unfolding.

The authorities stopped the river.
The third day of a trickle
to accommodate bridge building.
The bed is cracking, it stinks
like a sewer and ducks swim
in an ever narrowing stream.

It's hot and we need somewhere
to wade – but they have stopped
the river in the interests of
asphalt, concrete and traffic flow.

The studio is a hothouse.
I try to pick my best paintings
but the heat plays tricks on my
eyes, and all I see are rivers
and beaches, and waves stroking
shores.

After a time, the city's just so many warehouses
with wilting leaves and moldy cheese. We visit
the Queen of Kitsch, God love her,
clean up on half-price sales.

Clouds, you say? They let you know who's boss.
Coulda used some earlier, then late.
Almost running. Almost wondering,
talking and talking, listening,
hugging and hovering like apocalypse
waiting to happen. I'd rather be dancing,
but the microwave's the only one shaking
things up around here. I prefer lightning,
long strokes of electric cross my thighs,
stifled cries of burning. Is this how we die?
Honey, at every corner's a crane, metal bird
riding a tanned boy higher into sky to place
a sign: Affinity Bank. Higher and higher.
Here's the truth of space: the graffiti of my heart
is written, my mother is blind,
and fire is a painting in my mind.

    The river has been stopped.
    I run, then walk along its
    cracked shores, wonder how
    to make myself lighter,
    reduce my load.

    Far off, dear Terry is boxing
    the kitsch that filled the China
    cabinets of the old place.
    The Avon Corvette Stingrays,
    the porcelain belles
    and teddy bear bubble bath.

    Cheryl sends pictures of the
    renovations, of the newly

Open Up The Sky

emptied rooms, renewed floors,
smoothed walls.
The old place is empty for now.
I look out at the emptied river.

Graffiti sings on lathe and plaster.
A no neck monster and a big lipped girl
bawl and shout on rotting walls.
Here the church is sentinel over
a heartless town, the writing
scratched on a wall: "I don't
live here anymore, and neither
do you."
The monster lumbers down a
sagging stairway. The girl's lips
sound a goodbye.

Pitch. Pass.
Groove. Swath.
I've given the paintings
names, and will send them
out in the morning.
There will be the requisite
perplexities over abstraction.
Someone will say, "I see earth
from far above."
I'm prepared for polite protest
over the lack of timeliness
and content.
Claire has written of their
temporal source: "Like a
landscape glimpsed
through a prairie fence."
I thanked her for entering them.

I can't say what depths are there,
how far the layers go,
or what reflections penetrated
the surface in the making.
Moves are made for
colour, simply
for line, simply
for placement, simply.
Order and design simply there,
arrived at by choice, action.
I look forward to seeing them
once they are on their own.
I hope they speak to me.

What speaks is the journey.
What speaks? The dead.
Just out of Thunder Bay
we stop at Terry Fox's shrine.
I stretch, but there's no way
to describe this inland sea.
Superior, then Huron, then Nipissing.
All the water! At Agawa, we stop
and he takes the steep incline
down to red rock, down to border
lands where pictographs speak
simple languages of courage and of time.
He takes a picture to bring me to my knees
again. I take a flower, red, like my life.
Desire for a rock inhabits my bones,
swelling. Inactivity melts into a hum
keeping time with the motor.

Open Up The Sky

We are never still, pass lakes
in the silence of the Soo,
Sudbury and you,
and finally find the river,
Ottawa, still flowing. Still moving.
Still.

Here, the medium is river. It is its own painting,
though I hang new ones on the blue-grey wall,
though I imagine softer greens. In our terra-cotta
kitchen I hang an African basket and think
patience. Margaret's mandala, house
after house after home, the circle, the circle.
We have names for colour, line and space,
for pictograph and hieroglyph,
for nuance, movement, the line.
Your lines or mine? Abstraction is
space that blurs the lines between the worlds.
Lines fill colour. We catch light, life,
like fireflies, dragonflies,
a hummingbird I saw by the feeder
at Middle Lake. Lakes, fishes,
sugar and red dye to catch sight
of a tiny bird: something in me boils,
something sighs and sights
for paradise, paint, for line.
At the end of every line, at the end,
lines:

"Order and design simply there,
arrived at by choice, action.
I look forward to seeing them

once they are on their own.
I hope they speak to me."

Lines, they speak. Speak to me.

There, the view can't be painted.
You would have skirted it at Espanola,
before the Spanish River and the
black hills of nickel country.
Beyond the wood-chip mountain,
the sulphur plume and stink
of the paper mill.
I wish I'd known. I would have told
you to get off the TransCanada
and drive until an ancient mountain range,
worn to the white bone, appeared.
Where the Massasauga rattlers are all that
remain of the strange creatures that
must have walked and swum there.

La Cloche. The Bell.
Only the eyes and heart can capture its soul.
Some old painters tried once and failed.
I tried once, and failed.

Not paint, nor even photographs can tell some stories.
He climbed down to the glyphs,
pictures on stones. I said, "It's amazing they left
those marks for the future." He laughed,
"They left those marks for the moment, not for us."
Both of us are right, I guess.

Open Up The Sky

What does anyone leave? A mark in stone,
a mark on earth, a wish to have taken time
for the road less travelled.
Hurried, we left east of Nipigon
in morning's grey gloom.
Thud of the wipers steady,
I drifted between the waking world
and dreams, sometimes opened my eyes.
Red rock, silver rock, black rock,
black fish, white fish, smoked fish.
At a tourist beaver lodge, I bought earrings
made of lures. He wore fur,
became a different animal.
I walked in fur-lined moccasins
on skin of a creature bigger than a house
and called them mine.
It seems there's peace there
of some sort, the peace of trees,
the peace of closure, the peace
of woodsmoke under a low canopy.
I half expected snow in July.
1500 kilometres in a day.
Too much.

Too much.
God leaned over, rested a hand
in a basin, raised rocks
over waves too cold for plunging.
Here is where heaven freezes over.
Here is where a fingertip equals
a small lake: Dad Lake, Mom Lake,
Baby Lake.
Lakes with names longer than tribes,
Michi-what? and Manitoulin.

In childhood, we took a short road
to the Island, met Debassiges
and their kin, danced on sand,
slept under sky or in small cabins.
They all fall down.
Do I imagine that I remember seeing
a silver snake in the water?
Do I imagine spirits amongst the birch,
white-shod like travellers?
These coats feel cool to the touch
of a waiting cheek, grow moss and lichens
I will never name.

Another journey, past Thessalon.
Another geography, the wide corner
between God's fingertips,
Superior become Huron,
Huron become Nipissing,
Nipissing yields to the baby finger
of a wide river. Bring the world
to hollows made by the palm
of God's hand.

About the Authors

Heather Cardin

Heather Cardin has been teaching English literature for over two decades, in several provinces and a couple of countries. She has both a B.A. and B.Ed. from U. of S., and a Master's in English from Carleton University. She has four published non-fiction books, and poems in several anthologies. She has short-listed twice for the CBC Literary Awards in Poetry.

Poetry has woven through her life from the lyricism of having a musical mother, through the years of teenage angst, to study, and then to writing, including a thesis on the works of Canadian poet Di Brandt. She has studied at a variety of poetry workshops, including short tutelage from Patrick Lane and rob mclennan; she is grateful to Amanda Earl at Bywords, Ottawa for opportunities to publish and read, and to Ursula Vaira, at Leaf Press, for her dedication to the craft. She's mostly grateful for the constant reading of poets, whose voices linger: weaned on Whitman and Neruda, she now enjoys Rumi, Mary Oliver, and Lorna Crozier, among others.

After writing this book, life took her back to Saskatchewan, but she anticipates retiring to be closer to family in Ontario. She and her husband Bernie have three wonderful grown-up children and two great sons-in-law.

Rob O'Flanagan
Rob O'Flanagan has been a newspaper reporter, a photojournalist and a columnist for nearly twenty years. He has won numerous Ontario Newspaper Awards and a National Newspaper Award. He is the author of the *Blown Kiss Collection*, a volume of short fiction that began as a CBC Radio series in northern Ontario. He writes, performs and records poetry, and is a visual artist. Raised on a farm in central Saskatchewan, he is a graduate of the University of Saskatchewan. He lives in Guelph and is currently writing a novel.